The Life I've Been Living

by

MOSES CRUIKSHANK

Recorded and Compiled by

William Schneider
Alaska & Polar Regions Department
Elmer Rasmuson Library
University of Alaska, Fairbanks
June 1986

International Standard Book Number: 0-912006-23-4
Library of Congress Catalog Card Number: 86-051263
Printed in the United States of America, by Printing Services,
        University of Alaska Fairbanks.

Book layout and design by the Institute of Alaska Native Arts.
Illustrations by James Grant.
Cover photograph by Robert Cruikshank: Camp on the Hodzana.
Cover design by Deborah Grahek.
Beadwork design based on beadwork done by Ruth Newman Cruikshank.

Original publication funds provided by the National Endowment for the
        Humanities and the Alaska Humanities Forum.

CONTENTS

PREFACE

When the plane arches over the last summits of the White Mountains and, still flying northeast from Fairbanks, begins to descend over the Yukon Flats, towards the village of Beaver, it is the vast expanse of the Land that first confronts you. You have left one mountain range behind to the south and, ahead farther north, you can see the great cloudy wall of the Brooks Range. But now, below and on either side as far as you can see, lie the great spruce forests and their restful meadows, the thousands of lakes, the twisting creeks, and the lost sloughs. Cutting a wide swath through the middle, sweeping from your right down from Fort Yukon and disappearing to your left beyond the western horizon, comes the River.

This is The Land and its River (or perhaps, this is The River and its Land). Each lake, each meadow, each section of the forest, each bend and bar of the Yukon has a name and a story given by those who have traveled on it and through it and who know it intimately. It is an intimacy that airplanes don't allow as they skim rapidly through the sky. You have to touch it and let it touch you to know it, to love it, to hear its stories.

Now your airplane is descending, aiming towards the small cluster of log cabins on the north bank of the River. Here is the village and there are the log cabins and the airstrip behind the village and, now, you are landing.

Aside from the cabins you notice only two other structures. One is the Episcopal Church on the riverbank and the other, on the trail that connects the runway to the River, is the school. It is significant for the village and the Land you have flown over, that these are the two most prominent buildings. They are also significant for the stories you are about to read and the life of the man who tells them.

Begin to walk down that trail now, from the runway to the River, and stand in front of the school. The sign, in the front of the school, in the heart of the village reads, "Cruikshank School."

The sign was erected in the early 1970s by the village and the Bureau of Indian Affairs, when Moses retired from work there. We were told then that it was the first time the B.I.A. had so honored a living individual. None of us were surprised.

You are about to meet this man. He won't tell you that they named the school after him when he retired or the effect his life has had on others, but he will tell you about dog teams and prospecting and falling out of riverboats.

Listen carefully to him, as carefully as a hunter listening to the wind, as delicately as a prospector washing the sand out of his pan, paying attention to what is said and unsaid, to catch a sense of what a remarkable man he is. For though he tells you the stories of his life, for the most part they are not stories about himself, but about the people he was with—and some of their names are those prominent in Alaskan history. He happened to be with them not through sheer chance, but because they recognized his qualities even when he was a boy. It will only be after you have finished listening, and are walking back to your cabin, and your head is full of pictures of dog teams winding down the trails and nights around the campfires, that you will begin to realize the breadth and depth of this man.

His stories hover in The Land like the ghosts of early morning mists in the fall. The landscape, as far as you could see when you flew (and even farther, past the horizons), is dotted with places where he camped, lakes where he hunted, creeks where he prospected, and trails where he drove his dog teams. The Episcopal Churches in villages along the Yukon and Tanana rivers were built by him, and started by the men he traveled with—Archdeacons Stuck and Drane, Bishops Peter Trimble Rowe and John Bentley, the Reverend Robert Tatum. From the Aleutians, to the railroad connecting Anchorage and Fairbanks, from one end of the Yukon River to the other, to the golden creeks high in the Brooks Range—he has been there.

The stories from his life he shares with you gladly, with great enjoyment and fondness as he remembers. They are told not to herald his own accomplishments, but to teach and to help...to help those who don't know The Land see what The Land means to those who live there; to help younger people know what it was like in the early days, so that they might learn; to help members of the Church know where their Church has come from, so that they might be thankful; to help his friend Bill Schneider, who has asked him to tell these stories; and finally, to help you.

Perhaps, while standing in front of the sign at the school in Beaver, a slight breeze begins to blow through the willows and you can hear, on the edge of the wind, a violin playing. Follow the music farther down the trail and come now to the community hall, where there is a dance going on. Go ahead and step inside. The lead couple has just stepped onto the floor. With infinite grace, with authority and dignity, Moses begins to waltz across the floor, his wife Ruth in his arms. Out of deep respect for him, and the chance to watch a master, everyone else is still sitting and watching the couple. Finally Moses looks over his shoulder and calls out for the rest to join in. With a smile of enjoyment Moses continues gliding around the room with his wife, leading, as he has for all of his life, the way for those who come after him.

The Rev. Scott Fisher,
Episcopal Diocese of Alaska
Beaver.
Falltime, 1985.

vi

The Life I've Been Living

*And when
Moses begins a story, his eyes
light up, he sits forward in his
seat and then he begins by saying ....*

You know, these things that I talk about, I actually experienced them in my life. I talk about how we travelled on the trail, how life was on the trail, and how life was in those early days. And in working early days with our ministers and with other work that I did, it's from actual experience. And, of course, I was lucky. I worked with people that I learned a lot from, people that taught me what little I know. Like handling dogs, there's lot of things to learn about handling dogs and Mr. Richard Hearn, Kobuk Dick, he taught me what little I knew about dogs. All I knew about dogs he taught me when I was a youngster.

And then, of course, our missionary preachers and ministers, they taught us what little we know about book learning, writing and reading. We learned that at the mission schools. And the most important people those days were Archdeacon Stuck and Bishop Rowe. He was the bishop of the Episcopal churches up here. But Archdeacon Stuck, he travelled all over the Interior. He went to every village. He travelled by dog team in winter and by boat in the summer, on the *Pelican*. He was captain of the *Pelican*. And I was just a punk kid in those days, and I worked on the *Pelican*, tried to learn something, how to operate it. And if you ever read one of Archdeacon Stuck's books I think you'll find in there where he fished a kid out of the Yukon River with a pike pole. Well, that was me. I fell into the Yukon one time, when we were pulling out.

And there were things we had to learn those days, like from my grandfather, Henry. You know when I was just old enough, I remember he tried to explain to me how to hunt moose. Stuff like that we had to learn out in the woods. You take a greenhorn, he'll chase a moose all week and never get on to it. But if you know how, why if there's moose there you'll get him in no time. If you know how to go at it the old-time Indian way, you know. You have to watch that wind pretty close and certain time of the day he lays down and you've got to know that. You have to be careful of the wind. If you're watching when you're tracking him, and if you follow him, if you do it right, you'll come right up and you'll see him laying down right there. And if you get up close, you make one shot, yeah. Otherwise, if you don't do it right, why he smells you and he takes off, yeah.

Grandpa Henry would teach us even while we were sitting down by the campfire. Right in the camp, he tell us what to do. Like a lot of those old people, they tell us about how the animals behave, you know. This particular evening they might be talking about a moose. Next evening or the next time they talk about it, maybe they talk about caribou, how they hunt caribou. And maybe the next time bear, or different animals, you know. In that way the kids learn. The old timers tell them what to do, you know, and then, of course, they go out with the old folks too and that way they learn.

One of my early recollections of my grandfather was right there at that fish camp above Fort Yukon. And I remember that was the time there was some sort of a stampede down river, and those stampeders were coming down in those "Yukon" boats they call them.[1] And we had fish camp there, and we had a lot of fish drying and everything. We had fresh fish. And my grandfather gave them fish and some of them paid for it but they don't have to pay for it. We just give it to them. We had fish cooked and everything, you know. Some of those stampeders are very fine people, and then, of course, you run across knotheads too. And they try to make trouble. Why the old man is right there with his 30-30. He told them, "You get back in the boat there." And they travelled too. They're half drunk at the time, you know. They probably didn't know what they were doing. But the old man had to bring out the 30-30 to make them move, yeah. That was on the Yukon. Above Fort

Yukon. I remember that well because I thought sure there was going to be a fight or something like that. But the old man didn't back down at all. He tell them to "get" and he had his 30-30 there, and he told them, "You get or else there will be trouble."

As I said, there was those outlaws that felt they could do anything they wanted, absolutely disregardful of the rights of, well, say the Natives, you know. They thought they could do anything they wanted. And they got away with a lot of that stuff except when they run across knotheads like my old grandpa. Yeah, he stood up for his rights. But I don't want to give the impression that the stampeders were all like that because they were some of the finest people in the world, some of those stampeders.

EARLY RECOLLECTIONS

As a small boy I remember my grandfather, my grandfather Henry and my grandmother. We lived with them out from Fort Yukon, you know, out in the woods. Of course, that's where we always have something to eat, those days, is out in the woods. And I remember my grandfather had, he must have had about four, four or five different type of shoulder weapon. Guns. They're all muzzleloaders. Some were used for getting ducks and rabbits and birds, you know. He used shot in those. Shot, just like in a shotgun. And then for the bigger, big game like moose he had this bigger bore sort of rifles. I remember there was, well some of those muzzleloaders were round balls. And then I remember one particular gun, it had rifling in there. That's the one he took particular care of because with that one he can place his shot where he wants. It's accurate, much more accurate than these other smooth bores. With these other smooth bores, those big round balls, you have to get right up to the moose. But it's better than a bow and arrow. But this one with rifling, even from fifty yards, he could drop a moose, you know. And in those days, fifty yards to drop a moose was quite a ways with those weapons.

And I remember that he had some that I think they call them flintlocks. They use a stone there and the flint. There's a place you put powder. The fire from your flint as it strikes that place there, it ignites that charge and that goes right through the hole down into the barrel. It ignites the charge there for the round in the gun. He had a couple of those flintlocks. But the others were more modern. There were those with caps on them, you know. They were smooth bore but they had caps. After you load up the gun, then you pull back the hammer and you put a cap right in the nipple there, yeah. And that was more advanced than these old flintlocks that he had.

6

Those were the first guns that I remember that my grandfather had and all the old-time Natives there. And then the other more modern rifles came in like the 30-30 and the 44's, and all those old heavy caliber rifles, close range rifles. And I remember he had one 30-40 later on when they came in, he had that. That was his favorite rifle, the model 1895 Winchester 30-40. Oh, that was, that was his pride and joy. Nobody ever touches that, you know. And he took awfully good care of those guns. They had to be cleaned. After he take them out—he'd go out hunting with them—even if he didn't fire a shot they got to be wiped out and cleaned and put away. He was awfully strict about that. Every gun had to be cleaned and properly put away and all the ammunition and everything had to be kept in a good, safe, dry place, yes.

Now you hear tell that Natives are very careless about weapons. Not those old-timers. Now just to give you an example of my old grandpa, that powder horn had to be in a dry place, hung where absolutely no moisture can get to it. And same way with his other equipment. Like his bag for caps, and all the other things that went with it. Like the patches and everything that went with loading up those old time guns. They were all in a certain place. Boy, you better keep away from there, the Old Man will jump you. Every Indian family, one of the first things they learn is to take care of that muzzleloader that the man in the family got. It's got to be treated right and nobody's to fool around with it except the man, the hunter there. It was given good care and any kids that were caught fooling around with it, they get a good whipping. Yes, oh yes. They took care of their weapons. I've never seen anyone that was more stricter than he was, than my old grandpa. Everything had to be just so with those weapons, you know. He took such good care of them. Oh, sometimes you couldn't help, you know, like when a gun fall out of the sled like the one that he gave me.

That was an old muzzleloader that somehow or another got out of the toboggan and it hit a snag or a tree or something and bent. The barrel got bent, and that's how come I got that. He filed if off just above where it's bent. Then that work all right. He gave me that one. I had that one for years, yeah.

That was my first gun, a muzzleloader, smooth bore. And, of course, I had no way to get powder except from my grandpa. Once in a while he would give me a handful of powder, you know, enough for a couple of rounds for my muzzleloader, and a cap or two. Me and my partner would go way out there someplace and we'd fire it. And then my partner, he would have some powder too. I don't know where he got it but I suspect that he swiped some from his daddy or his grandpa too. So, he had enough for a couple of rounds for himself too.

I remember one time, somehow or another he got a hold of quite a bit of powder, black powder. He had it in a little piece of rag. He got it out then and we went out there and he said, "I'm going to blow it up." So he put it down on the ground there. There's a little breeze blowing, you know. And in those days we had those sulfur matches; it comes in blocks. You break off one at a time and you light it. You have to hold it until it gets darn good. Well, he was squatting down there on hands and knees and he lit this match. Little breeze blowing, you know, made it hard to light the powder. Well, he had to burn I don't know how many matches until he finally got it to the powder and it went off right in his face. Then his face swelled up and just the tip of his nose stuck out I remember. Oh, of course the swelling went down in a couple of days, but his face was all swollen up; his eyes were closed shut and just the tip of his nose was sticking out. I remember that well. Sam Roberts, he was my buddy. We got into all kinds of mischief.

We would rob caches of raspberries. We would climb up the caches. I'd watch; he'd climb up. There's berries inside those birch bark baskets, you know. And then he got a handkerchief and he'd fill that up while I watched and then he'd climb down and then we'd go someplace and eat them. Those were some of the things we used to do. We would go around, play around, and every chance we get, we'd swipe powder those days. We were just small boys, about 6 or 5, something like that. We were just kids then. That's before I went into the mission there at Fort Yukon.

Then later on in the fall, that's the time people go out to get their fall meat, you know. Get out there early, early enough so that they get their moose just when the moose is turning fat and the weather is still good so that they could dry that meat. You got to dry it. You can keep it all winter, you know.

And I remember Sam Roberts' family used to go along with us from

Fort Yukon up the Porcupine, up the Porcupine River to the meat camps up that way. The people had to go out there so they would have something to eat for the winter. The whole family would go, dogs and all. Most of the people them days, real early days, had those great big canoes—what they call woman canoes. It is actually a freighting canoe, but they call it a "woman's canoe" because the women operated it. They all take off from there and they had to haul what little equipment they had. The men had their own hunting canoe. They're nice and light. One man, he can travel all over the country with it. That's the one man hunting canoe.

Of course the dogs, they travel out on the land and they swim. Some of them get lost but somehow or another they show up later on at the camp. We get up there in the fall, early fall when the people can get moose and then have time to dry it while the weather is still good. Of course, during the winter they hunt moose too and caribou and all that, but sometimes game is scarce and it is good to have on hand a lot of good dry meat. The people depended on that. And berries, people used to have baskets after baskets, birchbark baskets full of berries in the fall—cranberries, blueberries. They have a lot of that, yeah.

We would all be out there in the fall. And then my grandfather, oh he's a rifleman from way back that fellow. He would kill a bunch of ducks and geese with his muzzleloading shotguns, yes. That was ducks and geese. He was pretty busy hunting all the time from morning 'till night. He'd come back, his canoe would be loaded down with ducks and geese. That's good duck and goose country in the fall. You know how ducks are gathering up ready to go outside. Oh, my golly, he'd have, I don't know how many hundreds of them, fat ducks. The women folks, they prepared that. They dried it so it will keep. And the women folks, they pluck it, they singe it and they dry it. Every bit of that duck is used, including the feet. Nothing is thrown away. It doesn't spoil at all. And I'll tell you, a good fat dry duck tastes pretty good, yeah.

And in springtime I remember when I was a youngster there, I would ride behind my grandfather in his canoe, in his hunting canoe. Well I was just a kid, I didn't weigh much, so I ride behind while he's out there on the lakes. And we would come back loaded down with ducks. And did he have some kind of firearm? No, he had a bow and arrow, a

9

bow with a bunch of arrows. And his arrows were those blunt-headed ones, generally made out of bone.[2] Those were the ones that he knock over those ducks with. See he saved powder and lead that way. Not only him, but all the other heads of families do that. They all go out there and they kill these ducks with bow and arrows. That's what they used. I'd ride behind him and he'd paddle all around the lake until we just get loaded down, we can't hold no more. Then we head for camp.

Those days, you know, it's either feast or famine and those people, in the early days I'm talking about, these people depended upon the country to eat. So while there's a chance to harvest quite a few ducks, why they will. Not one go to waste. They clean the ducks and they dry it. They dry it and save that for times when there is nothing else to eat. The same way with meat, any kind of meat they get, they don't waste it. It don't spoil. Before it spoil they dry it, yes. Then their meat won't spoil; it will keep then.

They're taught not to waste anything, especially like animals that we use, animals that we have to kill to eat, small animals like ground squirrels, tree squirrels. On all the other small animals, there isn't a thing on that animal that goes to waste. Everything is used, same way right on up the line with bear and moose.

When you kill a moose now, there isn't nothing that you're supposed to waste on that, including the hoofs. If the family happened to have lots to eat, lot of game around to eat and they kill this moose, and they're drying meat, they get the hoofs, they get the sinew on there and cut out this bone and just the feet are left. They tie these sinews together, those four hoofs. They climb a tree and they put it up there, out there in clear view where people can see it from long ways. Now this is what the Natives used to do. And that will sound foolish now, to the modern day so-called "sportsman," but that's the way our people used to do. They put them up in the hills. Some starving people see that up there and they can go up there and they get the hoofs and they can boil it. They boil it soft and that probably would save their lives, yeah. So like that, they put them up there and the hoofs stay up there three or four years. It don't spoil, it just get harder. But you boil it enough and it'll get soft, yeah. Stuff like that, they stress the importance of saving everything. Not a bit of that moose is wasted. Not only moose, same is true for caribou, bear, sheep, all the animals that they need to eat. They don't believe in killing more than you can use. It will be there when you want it.

In the fall, before they start rutting, moose is in really good shape. And when you open the stomach, it's just pure white there, fat, you know. Oh, that moose is in good shape. There's some good eating there. And certain times, different animals, you know, certain times they're in good shape; that's the time they get them, yeah.

When I was young, in fall-time as I said, we'd go up the Porcupine River. And the men, they'd take off in their hunting canoes and just the women folks and the kids were left in camp. My grandma was there and she took care of the household. She'd see that the things are done on time. Oh, she was busy. She was the boss. Yeah, she'd look after everything and she'd look after the kids. And then she was quite a hunter, too. In these days, Native women had to be just like a man. They had to be able to handle a rifle, you know.

Of course, we had to have fishnets and we lived off fish and looked after the dogs. And I remember there used to be what they call stickmen.[3] They come in there at nighttime, in fall, pitch dark. They would whistle and they'd throw sticks and make all kind of noise. They scared the women folks. We wouldn't sleep at all. Anyway, finally all the women folks and kids, we would get in these boats. Besides those freight boats, we have what we call "Yukon" boats. That is a square-ended boat made out of lumber that they got from the old timers that came into the country. Well, there'd generally be four or five of them in the camp there. The women folks and the kids get in them and they get out there in the slough and tie on to the snags and spend the night there. And in the morning we'd go to shore 'cause in the daytime they don't monkey around, those stickmen.

And I remember they would be up around the bend from our camp, while the men are still hunting. They would have a big campfire there and then they would dance around their campfire. We would see them just as plain as can be, yeah. I was just a kid then, and I remember. I had the sawed off muzzleloader. I had that loaded but I never did use it on them. I don't know, if I had to I would have used it on them, but I was just a punk kid, you know. I probably would have used it all right if I had to.

11

Well, all the women folks they had some kind of a gun too. They have to have for protection. And I remember my grandmother, she had the old muzzleloader. And she doesn't dare touch my grandpa's. He was so particular. And then after the men came back, why those stickmen disappeared. We hear them once in a while, but they are not so plentiful as while the men were gone. But there were those men, those stickmen.

And then, we stayed there until the men came down. They came down loaded down with meat. They brought down the meat in moose-skin boats. It's easy, if you know how, you make a good frame, and you use this green moose skin, use that and it's water tight. You can sew it if you have to here and there and use grease in there to make it waterproof. And they can haul a lot of meat with it down to the camp. And then the women go to work. They got to dry that meat, dry that meat so that it will keep, won't spoil.

Oh, they used to bring down, I don't know, quite a bit of meat. And then meat, ducks, and all the berries that the women folks have been picking, we have to try to take all that back to Fort Yukon before freeze-up. We go back there, go back to our cabin. Then we got a cache there and we put everything away there. That's where most of the people stayed, right at Fort Yukon. But then, the men folks had to get out and trap you know, trap and get fur for traders.

My grandfather was one of the great trappers there in early days. He always caught a lot of fur. He trapped up the Porcupine River, yeah, way up. Sometimes he went way up to the head of the Porcupine. Later, that was taken over by his son, Paul Henry. In those days, you know the old-timers they didn't go at trapping like that later generation, like my uncle, Paul Henry. They claim that he was one of the trappers that brought in the most fur in the early days, in the early days of trapping.

Yes, he brought in so much fur every year, from way up where his father used to trap, you know, way up. Of course, he extended the line later on, my uncle did. He made it a year around proposition. My grandfather, he caught fur as he was hunting for moose, or snaring rabbits, as long as they get something to eat. He didn't go at it regularly like his son, Paul Henry. Of course, things were beginning to change over then too, you know. In later years people had to go out to trap to make a living, after my grandfather's day, yeah.

"Oh, that's one of those old freight boats that the Hudson's Bay Company used to have."

Grandpa Henry used to trade with the Hudson's Bay Company when he was a youngster. When he was a youngster that's the only trading they had, was from the Hudson's Bay.[4] They came from Old Crow, those Hudson's Bay people. They brought down the stuff on the Porcupine River. As a matter of fact, I think my grandfather worked for them, for the Hudson's Bay. He was a captain or pilot. They had a big boat, big poling boat, loaded down with freight, and they got men in there to line and pole and row, and one man he was the captain or pilot. That's my grandpa's job. He was the pilot on there. A lot of those old-timers in Fort Yukon used to work for the Hudson's Bay that way too, like David Wallis when he was a young man. I understand that he was a captain for the Hudson's Bay on the boat. When you're captain on a boat like that, you're the boss. What you say goes.

Not all the old-timers got along with the Hudson's Bay traders. Chief Christian saw that they were robbing the people right and left and so he thought he was going to be a trader, and so he did get stuff. I don't know how he got it but anyway he traded. But he didn't rob the people like those early traders did. You know, early traders had those great big old long muzzleloaders. In order to get one, the fur had to be piled clean to the top of the long-barreled muzzleloader, stuff like that. He saw that was robbing the people so he learned how to be a trader. And it seems that he was sort of an independent man, you know, and he started trading on his own. He saw the Hudson's Bay coming in, taking over everything. Well, he started out on his own. This is what I hear, you know. And, it seems like he was kind of on the outs at the start with the Hudson's Bay, with the boss, the factor, or whatever they call him. I understand that he had to go all the way to Nulato to get his stuff: tea and powder and lead, stuff like that, you know, that he had to have.[5] That's as far as he had to go to get it. And then, then he get some stuff from Indians that been down below and been on trading expeditions. They trade amongst themselves too, and he was good at that, you know.

Anyway, for years he was on the outs with the Hudson's Bay Company. And then another man took over and then they made up. That's what I hear. And then he got trading stuff from the Hudson's Bay Company and did a lot of trading for them too. That's what I understand. He made trips all over, went even out to the Arctic there, way up north

14

there around Pt. Barrow someplace. I've talked to people up in Pt. Barrow who remembered when Chief Christian was up there. They all remember him. He went up there to trade, and the way I understand it he's always kind of like on his own, you know. He went up there to trade and he would come back loaded down with fur, yes.

I knew Chief Christian ever since I was a youngster and lots of the stories I hear about him is stories that are handed down from way back and I just repeat what I hear. I don't like to say anything that would downgrade a man and I want to try to repeat things that I believe is true, so I'm just repeating things that I heard about him. I just barely remember him, yeah. He came in for the holidays at Christmas and New Year's to Fort Yukon. Those were big times of the year, you know, and everybody tried to get in for the Christmas and New Year's celebration. Big time then.

Well, I remember him. He came in to Fort Yukon from over in the Porcupine country where he was. He came in there and he was sort of all by his own. He did this trading. He learned that way back when he was a young man.

In that way he helped the people quite a lot. It seems that, well, in other words he was one Native who stood up and tried to stand up for his rights and not be pushed around like they did to all the other people. As I say, he's one of those knotheads like my Grandpa and Old Adam. They just stood up for what they believed was right. Chief Christian was a good man, yeah.

And he had this young man with him, a man that was with him for years and years. Gilbert was his name. And the two were friends and they worked together. In the early days, Gilbert, he was a steamboat man, but after that he switched and went over to Chief Christian. He was with Chief Christian for years and years and they worked together. They trapped and traded and all that. Chief Christian was good at trading. He was a businessman I guess. I understand he brought in a lot of fur.

But I remember my grandfather and them, they traded there at Circle, with Jack McQuesten, and at Fort Yukon with Harry Horton, Billy Moore, and Harry Berman. I remember Circle as a youngster. It was a place for the miners. I remember steamboats coming in there loaded

15

down with freight, you know. And then these wagons coming in from the creeks. They would load up these wagons with freight. I remember those. Of course, there was a lot of excitement every time the teams come in there. There was quite a lot of freighting going on there in the early days. They were freighting out to the creeks, out around Central, up in that area. They spread out all over. But Circle was kind of the supply center, just sort of a supply center for the miners.[6]

My parents were there but my grandparents were down around Fort Yukon area; they were fishing at that time, yeah. My parents just moved up, they just moved up there and then later on they moved down, down to the fish camp above Fort Yukon. Those days people move by Yukon boats, put everything in the boat and you float downstream.

My folks lived at Fort Yukon and they trapped and fished out from there and my foster father, he died early. My mother lived for quite a number of years afterwards and, of course, she passed on later on too. I remember we had our cabin behind Grandpa, my folks had the cabin right there.

And I remember one time up at Circle, I was still with my own folks, you know. I was just a kid, barefooted kid, running around there. Well, we were out there and oh, there were big wagons. We kids were all excited. Watching. And by golly, somebody grab me and put me under his arm. The NC store was right there.[7] This great big six foot guy, he had me under his arm. He went in the store and he told that clerk, "Give this guy a brand new outfit of clothes." So he did. And I got a brand new outfit—hat, even stockings and shoes, coat, everything. On top of that, I got a big sack of candy—that big. After I put on my new clothes, then I ran about two miles back to the village.

16

*"That's Mrs. Burke. I remember her well. She used to tell me,
'You talk English, don't talk Indian.' But she took good care of us.
She was a wonderful lady."*

MISSION SCHOOL

When I was a little boy, I think I was about five years old, I was going home—back to the cabin. And here was a bunch of boys of my age, you know. They were throwing rocks and sticks at a female dog that had a bunch of pups. And that dog was loose. Well this dog would run after them and then those boys would take off and run like everything. And then that dog would stop and go back to the pups, and then these kids would go right back, start throwing again. Well I was coming by there and I stood there and I watched them. I didn't throw any sticks or stones. They kept throwing and again the dog took off, and instead of running after those guys she took off after me. So I hightailed it for our cabin and the door was open. And just as I get up over the door, the dog grabbed me by my leg there. It's all chewed up; my muscles on my leg were all chewed up. And they took me right away down to the mission there where Dr. Burke was. And he said, we'll keep this fellow here. He's pretty well chewed up. So I stayed there and I couldn't walk for quite a while. But eventually it healed and it's as good as ever.

Dr. Burke came there in the real early days and worked as a doctor at the mission there. In later years he met his wife up at Allakaket and they got married and then they moved back to Fort Yukon where he was doctor in charge of the hospital that was eventually built there, that the church built there. He was well-known all over, the only doctor available in that part of the country. Anyway, Mrs. Burke and them, they decided that that's where I should be, to try to get a little schooling and stuff. And they talk it over with my folks and they thought that would be a good thing. So I was taken into the mission there and I stayed there.

After I got to be about eight or nine years old then I was sent to St. Mark's Mission. That's over in Nenana. And in those days, you know, there's not many schools where Native kids could go. There was the

18

"I remember the Yukon well. That's the one I came from Ft. Yukon to Nenana on."

Holy Cross Mission and then the new mission school at St. Mark's Mission, Nenana. And I was sent to Nenana there.

I remember getting aboard the steamboat *Yukon* there at Fort Yukon and riding all the way, all the way to Nenana on that steamboat. That was quite a trip for me. We travelled down the Yukon down to Fort Gibbon, you know. They call it Tanana now. Then we come up the Tanana River to Nenana. That's where the mission was. There was just a small Native village there, trading post, and the few mission buildings. They'd just started it, you know. I was about eight years old I think, eight, yeah. I remember there's another fellow with me at that time, Paul Williams. I wonder if he is still alive. But the two of us went together to St. Mark's Mission that same year.

The first year that I went to Nenana there, that was back in 1913. And Archdeacon Stuck had just gotten through climbing the mountain. And all those dogs were there. And I remember the boys that took part in the work there. You know, they helped the expedition by hauling freight and everything, way out there to the mountain. It took a lot of work. Let's see, there was John Fredson, Ala Kellum, and Esaias George, those three Native boys. They were the ones who freighted all spring. And then Esaias and Ala, they brought back the extra dogs and sleds and everything. And John Fredson was at the base camp. He stayed there with a few dogs and looked after the camp. The rest of them, Archdeacon Stuck, Mr. Karstens, Mr. Tatum and Walter Harper, they're the ones that climbed the mountain there, Mt. McKinley.[8] I remember them well. I had just gotten to St. Mark's Mission, Nenana. And they left all the dogs there. Of course, it was easy to get feed there, big fish camp right there. You know, those days at the mission, everything had to be done by hand. We cut our own wood, and ran fishwheels. We dried fish and we put up salt fish and everything for the mission school.

Yeah, we had to work. We had to get our own wood, and on Saturday why all the boys that were able to work, and even some of the big girls, they went out. And it wasn't too far out to the wood yard from the mission there. We went out with five-foot one-man saws and six footer saws and we had to cut our own wood, haul it in by ourselves. And we spent all that time then cutting wood and hauling it in.

My mother, she sewed all my moccasins and made mitts. That's what

"That's St. Mark's Mission and the old hospital building. Yes, we raised a lot of potatoes there."

21

we wore those days, you know. Parkees and stuff, all that she made. She made them all the time and she sent them to me. Later on, after I was settled there at Nenana, the big girls, they did the sewing. Those days, that's what we had to wear, moccasins and mitts and fur boots and stuff like that. And they wear out in time, you know, but the big girls at the mission there, they did the mending. They mended our moccasins and boots and mitts, patched up our parkees and stuff like that. We didn't have much, you know, everybody had to pitch in and work.

Of course, later on after the mission developed, that was sort of a headquarters there for the mission and the dog teams. That's how come I started to work with dogs. I like dogs, you know, and I worked with them and right away they made me "dog boy." So I cooked for them and I see that they're fed on time, and I had to see that they had good bedding. Each dog had their own little house made out of poles, you know. And once in a while we'd put in fresh bedding like hay. We used to cut hay and put up a lot of hay, just for the dogs, yeah. Hay is good, but after it gets too old it's not much good. So we take that out and we put in fresh hay. Oh, the dogs like that. That was my job, looking after the dogs.

And, of course, when you talk about dog teams, you always talk about the head dog in that team. That's the leader. And one of the best-known leaders in those days was Archdeacon Stuck's lead dog and the name of that dog was "Muk." Archdeacon had that leader for a number of years, making his visitations to all the interior villages, and this dog was well known. And every time he came to a village there, why even the young-sters knew that dog, "Muk." He was a well-known dog, and of course, he was a first class leader. A good dog out on the trail, that was Muk. And then when he was retired from work we kept him down there at Nenana for a number of years, yes. Everybody come out to the dog yard there to see Muk. And then people coming through Nenana, they all come to visit the mission there, and of course, they have to go out and see Muk.

I like to tell a little story about him. You know, it was in the spring of the year, the days were getting longer. Well, I had a good dog house for Muk. But it's too warm for him so he got to sleep outside. He didn't sleep inside his dog house. He slept out there where there's ice, you know. And one of the first things we did in the mission there in the morning when we get up, oh, everybody gathered together in the big room there, and we have our prayers. We sing a song and then we say a few prayers before we go on our daily duties. And we're all gathered there, the boys, the big boys, and the little girls and the big girls, all in different groups there, and all ready to say our prayers. And somebody heard Muk making noise. They look out, and sure enough, Muk was out there. Oh, my. golly, they all had to run out to see what was wrong with him. As I say, it was the spring of the year, and Muk slept out there on the ice. Well, his body heat melted the ice and then his tail froze to the ice. He couldn't get loose. Boy, everybody rushed out there to help him get loose.

The mission had a great big garden and we raised all kinds of vegetable and potatoes. Oh, a great big garden. And then they had two fishwheels running. We caught a lot of fish, all the fish that we could handle. There was a lot of big boys in there then. They worked, you know, we little boys too, all the girls worked too. Everybody worked. That was quite a job looking after all those fish. Fish had to be taken care of; they got to be smoked just right. They got to be turned at a certain time, otherwise they'll spoil. Yes. So there's quite a bit of work, but there was big boys there and they knew what they were doing.

Like in the morning, first thing, why we had to run a great big poling boat, that's the way we go across river. The fishwheels were across the river. We rowed across there. There's two places to row on that great big old poling boat. Well, it takes four of us kids, one kid to each oar, four of us rowing, you know. We furnish the power. Of course, somebody in the back there, one of the bigger boys was in the back steering. We get over there and check the wheel. And oh, we'd be loaded down with fish, three, four hundred fish, you know, loaded down. We come back across and we land right at the fish camp there, and then the work begins, cutting the fish and drying it, you know, putting it away. Some of the good fish, like king salmon, those older boys and girls, they cut it so it's good for people to eat. It dries and they cut it in a certain way. It dries just right for people to use it.

There's so many fish, they had to work fast. Well, they don't have to be so perfect with the dog fish as the king salmon, you know. But even

before we had a lot of dogs, and Mike and Shorty, our two dogs, I remember them well. Mike and Shorty, and we had three sleds.

And we went by the Knight's Roadhouse. I remember Mrs. Knight was there. Oh, my golly, Mr. and Mrs. Knight, we got to stop there. She got to feed us up, you know, feed up those youngsters. She check our foot moccasins and mitts, and everything. She was a great old lady that Mrs. Knight. We never forget her, yeah. Well anyway, from there up to Middle River, that's where the big camp was. And the next day we got up in there. Oh, the people took us in there and we filled up on fat caribou meat. We stayed there a couple of days and then we started back down, loaded down with all we can pull. So we started back down, loaded down. We come down, down by the Knight's Roadhouse again, and we stop there and have another good big feed. Mrs. Knight, you know, she had made pies and stuff. She knew we're coming back that way. We don't get very many pies in the mission, but she made them for us there. Boy, we really enjoyed that. I'll never forget Mrs. Knight. Mr. Knight was there too, and their nephew Mr. Henry Knight. He was a younger man. He was one of the stampeders around there. And I remember him well.

Well, from there it took us a couple of days before we got back to town with all the meat loaded down. We had enough there for all spring and some that we could dry. Them days we didn't have those freezers or anything like that. In order to keep meat you had to dry it. And those big girls there, why they cut that meat after it thawed, and then they dried it. That way it keeps, keeps a long time until the fish come along. I think we made that trip twice. Yeah, we did that twice. Of course the people, always when they came in from the hills, they brought in all that they could put on their sled for the mission and they give that to the mission school, you know. People did that, they did that.

A SUMMER ON THE *PELICAN*

I used to work on the *Pelican*. You know, that's Archdeacon Stuck's boat. They had to have a youngster there to do the cleaning and the work for kids. All the boys wanted that job, you know. But they said the one that made the best marks would get that job. So I studied hard. And I guess I made the best marks. Well, I got the job. The *Pelican* would come to Nenana and then I would get on there.

I remember the first trip we made. It so happened at that time there were some church dignitaries in Alaska. I think you'll find some in the records there, Dr. Chambers, or Reverend Chambers, and Dr. Wood and Bishop Rowe. These people were from the mission board out there in the States some place. They came into the country to look around, you know. And they were travelling on Archdeacon Stuck's boat. From Nenana we came up here to Fairbanks on the *Pelican*. I remember we landed here Sunday. It was early Sunday morning when we landed here and all the people were excited, these big church dignitaries and all. And everybody was busy, Archdeacon Stuck and Bishop Rowe, and Dr. Wood and these other people. They had to go to the church and all that. I kept out of the way.

They finally all left the boat, except Walter Harper. Walter Harper, he was the engineer and pilot of the boat. Well, he had to take off too. He was going to escort a young lady to the church service, so that left me alone. As he left, Walter said, "Don't forget now, you have to go to church, and it's right up there. You see it clear?" I tell him, "Sure, I see it, I'll go." "Don't forget!"

Well, he took off. Well, after everybody left, I kind of straightened things up a little bit and then I got ready. It's time to go to church. Bell ringing, so I cleaned up and I got up on the bank and there's a board-walk there and a fence there. So I was walking along to church and I heard somebody yelling, somebody talking. And I look around, look around, my golly, here was a bird talking, you know. Well, I hung on that fence, I forgot all about church. That was the first parrot that I ever seen.

And then from there, after the people ready to go, then we start back down the Tanana, all the way back to Nenana. And then from there we went down the Tanana clear to Fort Gibbon. They call Tanana Fort Gibbon those days.

Yes, we come all the way down there, come by all these villages. At every village, we'd stop and they'd hold services. People got married, or people got to be buried, or there is baptisms. Oh yeah, sometimes we stay one or two days in these camps. And those days people used to camp along the river at good fish camps, you know. You have to fish those days. And we stay there and they have services and all the other work of the church.

Oh, down at Tanana, I darn near drowned there. I fell off the *Pelican* right into the Yukon River but Archdeacon Stuck fished me out with a pike pole.

From Tanana we went clean up the Yukon, up to Fort Yukon, all the way up to Eagle. Yeah, they had a church there too. We made it up in there too. And then we come back down.

After we hit the Koyukuk we started up, went all the way up to Allakaket. Yeah, all the way up to Allakaket. That's the mission there at Allakaket and Alatna. And that's as far as we could go. We were lucky we had good water, you know. We were able to make it up there. That's where we turned around on this particular trip. And we started back down the Koyukuk until we hit the Yukon.

Well anyway, we would start down the Yukon again, way down to Holy Cross, and then we stay there a day or so. Of course, that Father Jetté was there those days, you probably heard of Father Jetté.[10]

Father Jetté and Archdeacon Stuck and those other high church dignitaries, those Catholic people there, oh, they do a lot of talking, caring about the mission work and church work and all that down there. Yes, and then we finally take off, and then we go all the way down to St. Michael, all the way down to the mouth of the Yukon, yes. We go across the bay down there, I remember.

27

When we got there, we didn't even stop in town. There's a boat, a steamboat was out there in the bay. So, we went right out to it, and the captain, I remember, he calls through the megaphone, "Is that Archdeacon Stuck?" "Yes." "We've been waiting for you here. And you got Bishop Rowe with you?" "Yes." "Yeah, well, we're waiting for him too." So, we kept the ship waiting until we got in there, and then they took off. That's the only transportation back to the states those days, is by boat.

Then Walter and I, we got back to town and had a big feed and a good sleep. Then we started up the Yukon. We had to beat the ice, the freeze-up. It's getting late in the fall. That's quite a trip, you know, that trip there.

Walter, he hardly slept at all. But I ran the boat while he slept. He knew where it's safe enough, where he can turn it over to me. I was just a kid, but he had to have his sleep. So while he slept, I ran the boat. And one time, I went to sleep. I was at the wheel. I was sitting on this high stool and the engine's right back of me there. Well, I went to sleep and I turned like that, and I turned the wheel. Down below on the lower Yukon those banks hang over in sheets, you know. That's tundra. They hang over in sheets, just like blankets hanging over. Lucky I hit a soft part of the bank. It didn't hurt anything. Anyway I fell on the engine. Walter came jumping in there. But everything turned out OK. Anyway, we made it back to Tanana before the freeze-up and Walter was able to pull the boat out there.

And then from there I remember I went on the steamer *Yukon* back up to Nenana, to get back to school. Those steamboats, they can travel even though there's quite a bit of ice. Well, that was a whole summer's trip right there, yeah.

PREPARED TO CARRY THE MESSAGE BY BOAT OR SLED

"That's the Pelican*"*

TRAVELS WITH THE MISSIONARIES

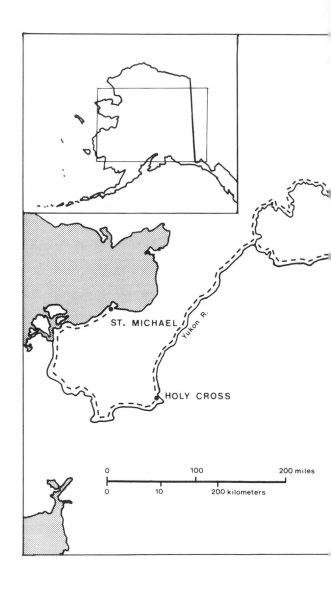

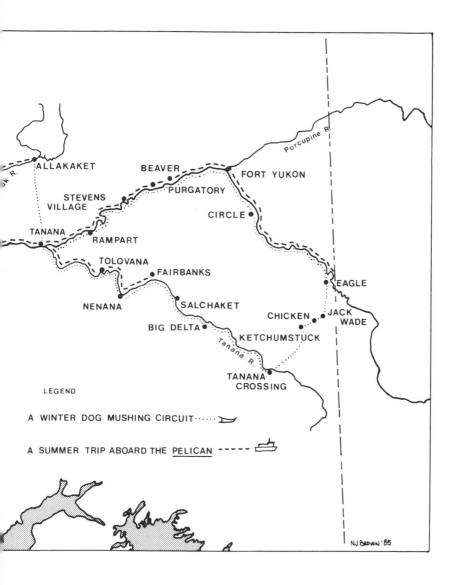

ALLAKAKET

BEAVER

FORT YUKON

Porcupine R.

STEVENS
VILLAGE

PURGATORY

CIRCLE

TANANA

RAMPART

TOLOVANA

FAIRBANKS

EAGLE

NENANA

SALCHAKET

CHICKEN

JACK
WADE

BIG DELTA

KETCHUMSTUCK

Tanana R.

TANANA
CROSSING

LEGEND

A WINTER DOG MUSHING CIRCUIT ·······

A SUMMER TRIP ABOARD THE PELICAN ------

N.J. BROWN '85

31

LEARNING ABOUT DOGS

As I said, at the mission, work was divided amongst the boys and the girls and my job all the time was with the dogs. I was interested in dogs. I like dogs, you know, and I took good care of them. So, that was my steady job, dog boy. I cooked for them and I fed them. I saw to it that they had good care. We changed the grass in their pen there every so often. And then in summertime, I saw that they got enough water to drink. So, I was interested in dogs as far back as I can remember. And then after I finished school there, that's the time our ministers made their visitations by dog team. And they generally had somebody along, a Native kid to go along to help on the trail. And that was my job.

I remember in the fall, I was told that I was going to travel with our minister that winter and we were going to organize a team. We had a lot of dogs there and some young dogs. And it so happened that's the time Mr. Richard Hearn came to Nenana. Like the rest of the old-timers, they all come to Nenana to look for work. They came from all over.

Nenana was a gathering spot for all the old-timers. They come in looking for a place to work, to make a grubstake so they can go prospecting. They come from the Koyukuk, Chandalar, way down the Yukon.[11]

Kobuk Dick came from the Koyukuk; he was over in the Chandalar. And when he got to Nenana there, he had his bunch of dogs there and he didn't want to kill them off. They were too good. So he sold some and then he donated the rest to the church there. And then he saw what we were going to try to do and he started to help me with organizing that team. Everything about that dog team he showed me. I was just a kid.

We started with the harnesses. In those days we used collar harness. We used dogs for pulling and the collar worked good. Each dog, each individual harness, he went over with me, to see that it fit properly.

And then our tow lines, neck lines and everything, he checked to see that they're proper length and all that. He went over the whole thing with me and then he helped me to train several of those young dogs. You've got to train them, otherwise you're going to ruin a good dog if you don't break him in right, yes.

Of course, a lot of guys they beat the heck out of a dog with the butt end of a whip. Those days in any of the stores you can buy these short whips, you know, and they got that butt end there. I don't believe in that, no. And same way with Kobuk Dick. He didn't believe in beating a dog. He says never use the butt end. Lot of fellows use that, that's no good. There have been a good many fist fights on account of that, those guys using the butt end and another guy trying to stop him, you know.

The way we stop a fight—we get that whip you see, and we double it up like this. And then, we have this loop right here, see that's just leather. It's not like the butt end that's solid there. Yeah, and then you stop the dog fight right there with it.

Then, as I said, Dick showed me how to break in these dogs, how to watch them. If a young dog don't behave right, sometimes you have to lick him a little bit and you have to talk to him, and then talk to him in a way that he won't be scared of you. If you use rough language on a dog, he'll get scared of you and he won't have no use for you, and he won't work for you! And he told me, Dick told me this, and he helped with the training of those young dogs.

And then one of the old wheel dogs,[12] Gunga Din, he's an old-timer this old wheel dog. He was a great big, powerful dog. He was a great big, oh, he must have weighed close to a hundred pounds, over a hundred pounds, powerful dog, wide chest, flopped eared, old worker from way back that one.

I had two, three young dogs we had to break in. And when we're out on the trail I have to holler at these pups. One young dog I especially remember, Monkey his name, full of mischief, you know. He wouldn't work. I have to holler at him. When we come home and I start to unhook the dogs, I start from the leader, and I unhook the dogs all the way down, and Gunga Din is the last one I take out. I guess he knew we were trying to break in these young dogs. He break away, go over and give this young dog a doggone good trouncing. But he don't hurt him.

And Dick said, "Let him go, he's learning them young dogs how to work." Yeah, he was quite a dog, quite a puller, a wonderful dog, old Gunga Din.

I remember one time going down to Tanana, I believe it was at Minto, at that roadhouse there. And the government team was from Tanana, Fort Gibbon, you know, the Army team. They come through there, and by golly we had this big dog barn in there, you know. We had our dogs in there. My dogs were all tied but the GI dogs, or government dogs were way back there, way back there. During the night, three of them got loose and they tangled up with Gunga Din, yeah. Gunga Din, he killed two of them and he crippled the other one so bad that they had to shoot him, yeah. And Gunga Din, he was chewed up too, but not too bad, he was still able to work.

We got that dog from Arthur Wright. He was a churchman and one of the earliest dog drivers for our ministers. Arthur Wright was the first one out on the trail with our ministers. And then he would train a team, you know, and that would be passed on to the mission. And he had a lot to do with the type of dogs. His job was to pick out dogs, work dogs. Great big, well built, powerful dogs you wanted in those days. He went from there out to Mt. Hermon, a school back in Massachusetts, the same school that Walter Harper went to. And that is the same school that John Fredson went to. When he came back, Arthur Wright went to work as a missionary and he married a nurse, Myrtle Rose, one of our missionary nurses, and then they had a family. I remember that well, 'cause I used to babysit their children Gareth and Don Wright. Arthur was one of the first ones, and later on Walter Harper, he travelled with Archdeacon Stuck for quite a while as his dog driver, you know. And then later on, Walter was with Archdeacon Stuck when they climbed Mt. McKinley. I understand he was the first man to step foot on top of Mt. McKinley. He was the athletic type, you know. Like at Mt. Hermon there, the records he made there, in running. He was a great cross-country runner. He made quite a few runs out there, and besides that, all of the other sports, he was up at the tops. He was quite a guy along that line, yeah, Walter Harper.

Anyway, as I said, Kobuk Dick been training me all this fall with the dogs and everything. And finally we were ready to hit the trail. And when we were ready to go he gave us his leader. You know, that's Molly, Siberian dog. Oh, that was the most beautiful dog I ever seen, spike eared, blue eyed, black and white spotted. Oh, she was a beautiful dog, ready to go. And if she's right at the head there, she jump way up in the air there and land on all four feet again, and she turn around and look, bark. By golly, that was a wonderful dog. Yeah, smart dog.

And Kobuk Dick told me, "Moses, on your travels you're going to find places where you're going to come out on a lake. The trail comes out there but there won't be a sign of trail there, and it's probably a couple of miles across over to the other end. You've got to find where that trail ends but there's no sign of it. You leave it to Molly. You just tell her to find that trail." And sure enough, more than once there's no sign of trail. And I tell Molly, "You go ahead." And she pick it up, a couple of miles over to the other place. She hit it right on the nose every doggone time, yeah! That was a wonderful dog, that Molly.

And then he told me what to do out on the trail, you know, how to take care of ourselves. Of course, those days they didn't have no airplanes or helicopters or Search and Rescue or anything like that. If you make a mistake on the trail, you paid for it. A lot of people froze to death on the trail those days. If you're not dressed properly, if you don't dress your feet or your hands properly, or any part of your body, you'll freeze. You have to be real careful how you dress. And he showed me a lot of things about that, about how to dress properly out on the trail.

And one of the things that I remember he told me. In the real cold weather, in real cold, fifty, sixty, or more, always have a bunch of shavings in the hind sack. What they call the hind sack in the early days, that's where you put things that you want to get at in a hurry. We always have a bunch of shavings in there ready, that dry, real dry wood. You can make good shavings with that, you know. Leave it there, it's just like coal oil. You can build a fire quickly with that.

And then he told me how to take care of the dogs when you camp at night. Fix up a place, be sure that there's no big lumps that they lay on. We generally shovel the snow away and then put spruce boughs down. He said, "Be sure that spruce boughs has no lumps, cut it up with your axe, cut it up small. He'll have a good place to lay down. If there's a lump there, they don't rest good that night."

I learned lots from him. One of the things he gave me before I started on the trip was trail mittens. I had my regular mitts but he told me, "Moses, you use this when it's fifty below or colder." It's a regular moose skin mitt and it's lined inside with fox skin, with the fur side out. And then on top of that it's filled in with small pieces of rabbit skin, dried rabbit skin. You put your hand in there and it's just like putting your hand in the oven. I use that only in cold weather, you know. Working around with the dogs and working in camp, making camp like that, it's clumsy working with mitts, so you always have gloves too, a couple of pair of gloves. Of course you don't want to get one too wet. That cold and that heat sometimes makes your gloves wet and you have to watch out they don't get too wet. Be sure to have dry gloves. But after you get going on the trail and you're riding, why you wear these big mitts, yeah. But working the dogs, we always use gloves, dry gloves.

And then another thing is your footgear. You have to be awfully careful about your footgear. Always have an extra pair of boots in the hind sack. You generally have insole socks or socks made out of caribou skin. Native made caribou skin socks, they're worn inside your boots, yeah. And then the best boots we found for use out there is this canvas boot. Of course, fur boots is all right for some people. But certain times of the year fur boots will frost up inside during the day and then towards evening, if you don't change your boots, you're going to freeze your feet. That's why that canvas boot I believe is the best. I explained that to the service when I was in the military.

You know, when I got in the service there, I noticed a lot of the stuff that they had there wasn't quite adequate. So I wrote home to my sister and I got my boots, canvas boots, and my mitts, my loose gun case and stuff like that. And then when I got them, I showed it to these big shots. Oh, they called special meetings and they talked about it and I explained to them all that. The outcome was that, finally, they worked out some kind of a scheme where the Army adopted those canvas boots. But I told them, "Not oil tan, it's got to be all dry tanned. With oil tanned you'll freeze your feet. It's got to be dry."

And then the loose gun cases for our rifles. If we didn't have no case at all, why snow would clog up that darn automatic gun in no time. With a loose gun case, you just slip it on, that's the kind we use hunting

36

out in the woods, the kind we always put on our 30-30's to protect them
from snow. And it does protect them from snow. When you're ready to
use it, just slip it off. Your gun is in first-class shape, ready to work.
They did work out some kind of a loose case too. And then they came
out with some kind of a version of the mitts, tied around your neck, you
know. They had that too.

One thing I tried to explain to them those days was that you've got to
have those big mitts. When you're working outdoors, you got to have
gloves. Now, like working in the Army, you know, like those gunners,
the machine gunners, those guys with light guns, things like that. You
can't wear those great big mitts, it's clumsy. Tie them on a string so
that you can tie them back there and wear gloves. When you got time,
put your gloves inside your parkee pocket and put your hands inside
those big mitts to warm them up, keep them from freezing. It's just like
an oven. That's how we work it at home. I told them a lot of things like
that. I don't know. Well, they might have adopted some of the advice I
gave them. Anyway, I'm glad they adopted those big mitts because I see
a lot of the Army is using them now.

MUSHING WITH THE MISSIONARIES

Well, back to mushing with the ministers. I travelled with the Reverend Tatum, and I travelled with Reverend Drane, and then I travelled with Reverend Bentley just before he was Bishop. These were three that I remember well. That was on the winter trail. We would start from Nenana on the old winter trail, on the old mail trail. Those mail carriers, they were the ones that kept the trail open. They had to carry the mail by dogs and no matter how bad the trail is, they had to get out and break trail. A lot of people used to wait for them to break trail, unless of course there's a stampede someplace, then everybody is going to break trail.[13]

Anyway, from Nenana we start down this way, all the way down to Tanana. The preacher that I happened to be travelling with at the time was Reverend Tatum. And he had a brother who was stationed there at Fort Gibbon, a Lieutenant Tatum. So when we come through there with the dog team, why they invited us down to the post as guests. And that was the first place that I ever seen a moving picture. And I remember that it was run by Mr. Al Rowe. Mr. Rowe was in the Army at the time and in later years, quite a number of years afterwards, Mr. Rowe finally settled up there at Fort Yukon and he ran the generator house there for the mission and the hospital. He was a first-class mechanic and he kept things running. He had a power plant there and that was his job for years and years. He was well-known and loved.

Then we come over the winter trail, over toward Allakaket. The old winter trail used to go over that way. We go overland on the old winter trail. And then from there the trails go to Bettles, Coldfoot, and Wiseman. Then we'd start back down, back to Allakaket, and then back across country over to Tanana. After we get back to Tanana we rest the dogs for about four or five days, you know. We get them in good shape, feed them good, and give them a good rest and all that. And we rest ourselves too. Anyway we start up, start up the Yukon.

I remember the first day out from Tanana, Jordan's place. I wonder if any old-timers remember that, Jordan's. I guess Mr. Jordan was one of the real old-timers in the country. Of course his son Charley, Charley Jordan, I remember him well. How many of those boys still live I don't know. But I remember Charley well. And Mr. Jordan, of course he's gone now, but he's one of the real old-timers. He had a place there, sort of a roadhouse and he cut steamboat wood and they has a horse there.

I remember that was the first roadhouse and then we used to go all the way up, all the way up to Rampart. And I remember we stay there. Quite a few people there, you know. People got to be baptized, church work to be done. A lot of the old-timers were there. The Mayos were there. I remember old Cap Mayo, he was still alive. And quite a lot of the other old-timers were there.

Old Cap Mayo had a big family there and there's a lot of his children. You hear a lot about Mayos, they're all over, yes. But I remember Old Cap Mayo, he's one of the real old-timers. He was an old man, and me, I was just a punk kid, you know. John Duncan was the man that ran the NC store at Rampart, in those dog team days. I had work to do there. I had to cook for the dogs and look after the dogs and all that while the preacher goes in there. He talks with the people, all these old-timers. They hold services and married people that were getting married and baptized people and some places have funerals, you know, when people died, passed away.

And then we start up, all the way to Stevens Village. I remember at Stevens Village, that's where Henry Moses worked for the church there, a lay reader, you know. And Miss Harriet M. Bedell, she was charged with the church there. And that's where I first seen Harry Moses and Mabel Edwards, his future wife, there at Stevens Village. That is where they got married. And I can remember when they were married, Reverend Drane married them. How many years was that? Sixty years, sixty-five? Yeah, there was some kind of a celebration for them here in Fairbanks, quite a while back.

Anyway we'd start up from Stevens Village and go up to Purgatory. The Yanerts settled there at Purgatory and they had a nice cabin there.

*"Henry Moses and his wife Mabel and Miss Bedell. Deaconess
Bedell, yes. She was in the Mission Service for quite a number
of years."*

Oh, they had a wonderful place. I remember driving through there. The trail come up on the bank, oh, probably about a mile below. And then we come out through the timber. They had a good sheltered place there and a good area for a cabin. And we come out there and here by golly, there was a moose right out in front there. Of course, my team made full blast for that moose. But I had a good leader and we got the dogs away from there. The moose was stuffed! But the dogs see it, you know, see it in the yard and they all go for it. And by that time Mr. Yanert came out. He had that moose mounted in the yard as a joke. He came out there and he helped me, helped me put away the dogs, helped with everything. That's the time I was with Reverend Drane, back in 1920, I think. I'm not sure about the year, but probably around 1920.

We generally stopped couple of days there to rest up the dogs. And Bill Yanert, he wants us to stay, yeah. He got somebody to talk to, you know. And Herman, his brother, he helped me cook for the dogs, look after the dogs. By the time we got there, our supply of beans was getting low and Herman, he helped cook up a fresh batch of beans. Them days, beans were the standby on the trail, you know. You boil them until they are done, then you drain the water out of it, and you spread out the beans on a piece of canvas. And just as soon as they dry, you gather them up and put them in a fifty pound flour sack. If you got two fifty pound sacks then you'd be doing good, yeah. You just put them in the sled. A handful of those beans and a chunk of boiled moose meat goes pretty good, yeah. And we always stay overnight with them there. And sometimes they talk the preacher into staying over an extra day to rest up the dogs.

He was quite a man, Mr. Yanert. I understand that he came up here in the early days on sort of a survey expedition.[14] I think he was in the cavalry. And Herman, Herman Yanert, he was an infantryman and I remember him telling stories about that. After Bill was retired, he came back to the country and settled in there, and later on his brother Herman joined him.

That was their headquarters cabin at Purgatory. From there they trapped, you know. They didn't use dogs. They pulled everything by their neck. And they travelled, they had a lot of cabins all over. They trapped on the Hodzana and on the Yukon too, and in this area between

41

the Hodzana and the Yukon. All this area in here is where they trapped, yes. There's good marten country in there and they covered that pretty well, yes.

But I remember them well. We stopped there the time I made that trip with Archdeacon Stuck up the Yukon. We stopped there and it was all we can do to pry Archdeacon Stuck and Mr. Yanert apart. They talk, my golly they talk about things up here in Alaska, you know, about the people and everything else. I never seen two people that could talk so long as they did. They were good friends.

On the river bank there, they had something rigged up and you touch the lever, why here comes a great big image of, I don't know, they call it the devil. It jumps right out of the ground. I remember that quite well, especially later on when I travel on the boat, working on Archdeacon Stuck's boat. I used to spring that lever there so I can see it jump up. I was just a kid then. Anyway, we stopped there at Purgatory, rest the dogs and fix up beans for the trail, and then we start up to Beaver.

At Beaver, I remember Mr. Yasuda. Mr. Frank Yasuda was one of the old-timers there. He came into the country in the early days with his wife Nevalo.[15] And Mr. Charlie Schultz was around Beaver in those days. He was in the freighting business. He had a bunch of horses and he freighted up into the Chandalar and the Koyukuk on those old wagon trails. And I remember he had a bunch of horses there and wagons, everything. And then another character there was Mr. French Jim, they called him, James DeSarmian. I think that was his name. He ran a road-house there and a bakery.

Another man there, a Native man was James Pitka. Of course, you heard about the Pitka family, a lot of them around now. But he was their dad, old James Pitka. He was quite a character. He was well-known and liked by everyone. And then there was the Hope family. They came in there in the early days. And then of course there was Turak Newman. He was one of the people that came into Beaver from Wiseman and from the coast there early days. He's well-known over in that area. He raised a big family and I'm married to his daughter, Ruth. Turak Newman worked for years over in the Chandalar as a miner. He had the reputation of being a first-class miner. He's one of those guys that just knows just where to put your point and everything like that. He's one of

*"That's Bill and Herman Yanert. I stop there at that cabin a good
many times."*

"Yup, that's the devil at Purgatory."

those guys that just seems to know just what to do. Everybody wanted him to work, work for them, because he was a good workman. Anyway, he was working for Mello and Mr. Mello was just about ready to quit, you know, and Turak told him it looks good so we'll put in one more thaw. Turak drove in the point there and when they clean out that thaw, that was one of the richest discoveries they made over in there. From that discovery, that's where Mr. Mello made a stake.

Well, after we left Beaver, we go all the way to Fort Yukon. At Fort Yukon there was a big mission station there. We stay there about four or five days. After the dogs are rested up and we are rested up ourselves, then we start up. Then we come to Circle, still following the Yukon River. Those days there is trail on the river. Everybody used the dog team trail, you know. That's what everybody used. We had a church there at Circle too and we stay there a couple of days. Then we start up, go all the way to Eagle. And there's a mission station there too. Oh, we stop there for two or three days.

Then after we rest up there and get ready to hit the trail again, we make sure that we have enough beans and bannock cooked, you know. Bannock, if you cook it just right, it will keep a long time; it doesn't freeze too solid either. It's good.[16] Well, we start out from Eagle and then we head up toward Ketchumstuck, Jack Wade, Chicken, yeah. That's quite a trip coming over this way, you know. There was some people up there, miners, our church people. Women folks, they want us to stay there. Of course they feed us good. Anyway there was probably some people to get married or kids to be baptized. We eat good. Those women folks, they take good care of us there. And after that, we started up, and we go to Ketchum Village, Ketchumstuck Village.

And about the first time I seen a coyote…it was up in that country. Early days they didn't have no coyotes here in the country. Those days out on the trail, there used to be a lot of caribou in the country, oh thousands, countless caribou those days. And sometimes in some of those lakes in the area you find a lot of dead caribou, killed by wolves. It seems like they just kill caribou just for the sake of killing. When we come to find some caribou like that, generally they're sour by that time, but they're good dog feed. We cut up a bunch of them and put them on the sled and feed the dogs, give the dogs a change in feed and they like that feed too, yeah.

45

"Turak Newman worked for years over in the Chandalar as a miner. He had the reputation of being a first class miner, and he's one of those guys that just knows where to put your point and everything like that."

And as I said, there was all kinds of caribou, and I remember way up at the head of the Tanana, I forgot where it was, I think it was on Lake Tetlin, we were going along and here I see something crossing the trail. Well, one of the things that I did when travelling on the trail was to have my rifle there, and any fur I got, I could use, I could turn into money, see. I knew that. So, I look and I said, what in the world is that? It looks different from anything I've ever seen. I said, that couldn't be a wolf because it's so small. If it is a wolf it must be a real small one and it's not a...It could be a big old red fox the way it look from a distance, you know. By golly I didn't know what it was. Anyway, it was getting away, so I grabbed my rifle and I shot and knocked it over. I went up there and picked it up and golly, I didn't know. I looked around for a dog team, I thought that it was a dog. I looked around and said we'll pay somebody for a good dog. There was a cabin at the other end of the lake. So I threw that animal on the sled and went to the cabin there, and here was a Native and John Hajdukovich. He was a trader up there. That Native driver, he was freighting for him and I asked him, "What's that?" He said, "Yeah, that's coyote, coyote."

I don't know whether any old-timers remember this or not but I'm sure they do. Those years, we didn't have coyotes in the country. For years and years we didn't have coyotes, then all at once they moved into the country and there were a lot. I remember that was the first coyote I seen. I was young that time travelling with Reverend Drane.

Sometimes we hit cold weather, fifty below, sixty below. Why, it's foolish to travel in cold, real cold weather. It's too dangerous. When we hit a cold spell and we happen to be in an area where there's a lot of dry wood, we camped right there; we stay right there until the cold spell is over. We always were loaded down with grub, you know. We carry all the grub we think we need, and extra too if we can. But we don't want to overload the dogs. We have to watch that too. We have to carry food for our dogs, so every pound counts out on the trail.

On a typical day we would start out early in the morning, go ahead with the dogs, dog team loaded down. Our minister, he's holding the handlebars, riding at the handlebars. And me, I'd be at the gee pole.[17] In those days we had long basket sleds. They were limber as a snake. They followed the trail. That's different from the sleds they have now, those short sleds they have nowadays. We had those long limber 14, 16 foot sleds, Native made. And in front we had that bow there and there's a seat in there made out of babiche.[18] I would sit on this babiche chair and I had short skis on my feet and I had this short gee pole and guided the sled, kept the sled on the trail with that short gee pole. And the minister, he hang on the handlebar behind and we would travel that way.

Noontime, we stop at a good place where there's a bunch of good dry wood and build a fire and make tea and have lunch. The dogs get a little rest. We all get a little rest and then we start off again. Then we always have to find out ahead of time where's a good place to camp on that trail. You get that from people along the trail that you know. They'll tell you a good place to camp. And sometimes if you come a little early, why camp anyway because you can never tell when you'll find another good place to camp. A good place to camp is where there's good dry wood, see, a lot of dry wood there. That's the main thing—dry wood and spruce boughs. And the first thing we do is pitch up the tent, get our snowshoes and shovel away the snow down to the ground. And then we put down spruce boughs, pitch up our tent, rig up our stove and then bring in the stuff. By that time I have a few blocks of wood cut, dry wood to start up the fire in the stove. And then we bring in everything that we need for that night. Then the minister, he starts cooking our dinner. Me, I start cooking dog food.

I build a campfire out there and we have our own dog bucket, cooking pot. In those days, the blacksmith in any one of these mining camps, they made dog pots to carry on the trail, and they fix it so it will fit in your sled wherever you want that load. They fix it the way you want it. And then on top of that we had to carry these basins that fit inside each other so each dog had his own individual dish. So, while the minister's cooking in there, why I start up the dog feed.

I start a campfire and put my dog feed on there and melt snow. As soon as it is melted, why I put in my fish. And as soon as it start boiling, then I put in the rice. Rice and fish we cook. We know just how much to put in there because we done it so many times, you know. Sometimes you don't put enough, it's just thin, it's no good! And sometimes you put too much, it burns. Dogs don't want burnt feed. They don't want to eat it. So you have to watch to see that you have the right

amount of fish and right amount of rice in there. And don't burn it!
Yeah.

As soon as that feed is done, why then I ask the minister to help me.
We take off that dog feed and put it in the snow there so it will cool off.
And by that time the minister has everything cooked so we go in there
and then we have a big feed. We'll have a feed and then we wash the
dishes and put things away. Then I have to study for about half an hour,
reading, writing, arithmetic. I got to study that. But, before we start, we
go out there and the dog feed is already cooled off some. So we get all
the dog pans and we dish out the feed into each individual pan. And
then I would get the tallow and put the same amount of tallow in each,
in each individual dog pan. That way each dog will get a fair share of
tallow. Sometimes they used to put tallow right in with the feed but it
don't seem to work good that way. If you want to be sure each dog gets
his full share of that tallow, you put it into each individual pan. But the
feed is still warm, hot yet see, so we leave everything out so it will be
cool. The dogs are sound asleep. They know it's not time to eat yet.
And then we go back inside the tent there and start my study. I study
for maybe half an hour or more, sometimes more than that, and by that
time the dog feed is cooled off enough so we can give it to each dog.

We go out and give each dog his pan. In that way it's not too hot, it's
just right. And you don't want it too cold either. You want it just warm,
you know, just warm. It's good for them when it's warm. You have to
give it to them just when it's right. Oh boy, they like it then. Then we
go back inside the tent and I close up the tent real good for the night
and put in a couple of big chunks of wood inside the stove, adjust the
draft so it will keep for a long time and make shavings and everything
so we can have fire in the morning. And after that we say our prayers
and then hit the sack. And it seems like I just get in the sack and get
straightened out and then I hear the alarm going off! That was a typical
day out on the trail.

Them days we don't make long runs, but, of course, nowadays they
travel a long ways. For those days, seventy-five miles was a long run.
My dogs were toughened in, tough as could be. They were travelling all
winter. And they were in good shape. In springtime, when good conditions, all I had to do was ride.

49

Anyway, we would wind up at Tanana Crossing. See, they called it Tanana Crossing those days, Tanana Crossing.[19] We had a church there and we'd stay and rest up a few days and treat up the dogs.

Then we started down. By that time, it's spring, you know. Yeah, by golly, sometimes we have early spring. And if you get early spring you better get back to where you are going before the snow all melts. Well, sometimes I'd be lucky and we'd have enough snow. We start down the old trail. I remember all those villages—Big Delta, Healy, Richardson, and there used to be a village out there, Salchaket, that's it. By golly, sometimes it's getting late, rivers breaking up. It's soft and you have to be doggone careful.

At Richardson there, that soldier that was on duty, he can see up the river quite a ways, you know. And he see us coming. He see us coming from the cabin. He look, he look up there, he see us, and then he went and did something, go to work. Next time he look, here the whole dog-gone river was open. It open up after we pop by there. Anyway, he had all the people all excited by the time we got to the village. We got there OK, but he thought that we got lost there, which we could easily have done. Because the thaw in the spring of the year, when the river start to go to pieces, why you hit soft spots and down you go, and that's the last they'll see of you, dog team and all.

And then from there we start out for Fairbanks, and we get back to Fairbanks on the last snow. That would be the end of our trip right there.

Well, those days we landed in Fairbanks right below the church and there was a board sidewalk there. There were a few large buildings but most of the buildings were logs, log cabins, log buildings. Then of course when we used to mush in from the trail, like coming in from the head of the Tanana River, we would come into Fairbanks and we would sign in at the Pioneer Hotel. We stop at the Pioneer Hotel and then we take the dogs down to the big barn there and we put the dogs away. Dogs and horses stay in this barn. You had to keep your dogs well tied, have good snaps on them. And they did have good snaps those days. Things were made good those days, you know.

And after that, why we would go back and wash up and then we would go to that Model Cafe.[20] All you can eat for six bits, yeah. That's the way it used to be in the early days.

Those days they just built that Alaska Railroad and they had that narrow gauge between Fairbanks and Nenana. I remember we shipped our dogs to Nenana. Sometimes there's no more snow down there. All the snow was gone. That was a winter's trip. It took all winter, yeah.

"That's the old Pioneer Hotel. We used to stop in there quite often."

"And after that, why we would go back and wash up and then we would go to that Model Cafe, all you can eat for six bits, yeah. That's the way it used to be in the early days."

*"These are the travelling sleds, as limber as they can be, all tied
with babiche, with give to it."*

WAGE WORK

After travelling all winter long with our minister, we'd get back to Nenana on the last snow. And my dogs, they are all toughened in. They're really in good shape. And then Mr. Hagen would come up and talk to our minister and they want to use me and the dogs. Mr. Hagen, he was the Deputy Marshal down around Nenana area. And Mr. Senafe was the Prohibition Agent, I remember them. They were up in this area—around Nenana.

So I took Mr. Hagen and Mr. Senafe, and we'd go out. We'd have to travel nighttime because the snow is real soft, and nighttime it froze over real good. Then you can travel anyplace with a dog team. We had those long basket sleds, you know, travelling sleds, freighting sleds, Native-made sleds. They're light and they're limber as could be. We take off from Nenana and we go out and then they'd make some arrests, I remember. They had all kinds of evidence that I had to haul in, you know, the stuff they make booze with, what they call the coil or whatever they use.

All that I have to load in there. And then I remember they took one guy in. They thought they might have a fight with him there but they got him all right without having to shoot. I remember them checking their guns before they went in after him. Anyway, we gathered all that evidence and them two riding on the sled and me riding behind on the handlebars. We were loaded down. But as I say, good travelling, everything froze solid, nighttime, you know. The dogs were in first-class shape. Oh, we travelled. So, I put in quite a bit of time working for Mr. Hagen and Mr. Senafe. And all this money that I got from them, that went toward my schooling at Mt. Hermon, in Mt. Hermon, Massachusetts.[21]

And summertime, I work on the railroad. That money I made, that

55

"Yeah, that's the surfacing crew building the old Alaska Railroad. I was water boy on the surfacing crew."

"Well, that's the power they had those days—horses and mules.
We didn't have no big earth moving equipment."

"That's the way they used to lay rails. Then the spike boy comes along and he lays down spikes. Then the spikers come behind."

goes into my schooling too. I didn't make much money. I got seventy cents an hour, but them days seventy cents went a long ways.

I worked on the Alaska Railroad when I was twelve years old and I worked as a water boy, water boy and spike boy.[22] You ask any of the old-timers and they know what that means. Of course, nowadays, these people don't know what in the world those mean, spike boy, water boy. Those days, that's before they had these big earth moving equipment. There's no tractors and no big caterpillars. It's all horses and mules and big gangs of men with picks and shovels. I worked in Old Martin's gang. I think a lot of the old-timers can remember Old Martin's gang. That's a surfacing crew, you know. They work just ahead of the steel gang, getting the roadbed ready. And then the steel gang comes behind laying down the steel. Old Martin was the foreman. He must have had at least two hundred or more men working on that. It was all hand work, pick and shovel and horses and mules. A lot of the old-timers came there to work, you know, and Mr. Kobuk Dick, he was a good man with horses. He got a job there as teamster.

People were coming in from all over looking for jobs those days, summertime, you know. And I put in two or three seasons working for the railroad there. I started out as a water boy, finally wound up as a laborer, seventy cents an hour, yeah. But them days, a dollar went a long way. When I first started out I was twelve years old, worked out as a water boy.

I remember those big gangs of them. Old man Martin, he was a strict old son of a gun. Well, he was a good man, he knew his business and he had a big gang of men there. And then later on I worked the steel gang as spike boy, Lee's gang. Some of the old-timers remember Mr. Lee, he was the boss of the track layers, those guys that lay the rails and spike it down to the ties.

And then during the years, like in 1920 and '21, I had other jobs too. They shifted me around all over. I worked down at North Nenana and then I worked on this line that they were building here to Fairbanks. I worked on a freight train, what they call work train. We used to haul in logs from Dunbar to Nenana. The government was building a sawmill there at Nenana at the time and we were hauling these logs there. Oh, we got a big pile of logs there. Anyway, finally when I was laid off, I got a job on that government sawmill. I worked there under Mr. Head. He was the boss. He was the boss sawyer. And I work there for all summer. One of the guys that worked there was Harry Riley, you know Harry Riley? He was there.

Harry Riley is an old friend of mine. We went to school together there at Nenana in the early days and then we worked on the railroad together, and then we served in the military together too. He was drafted into the service too. So, he's an old friend of mine.

Then I worked here and there, transferred here and there. Four years I worked for the railroad. But, I don't know, somehow or another the records are all fouled up. Now, they have absolutely no record of me at all. And I have a lot of affidavits signed by people that knew me and worked with me when I worked the railroad those days. And we sent that out to Washington. They tried to give me some more time on my pension, but those people out there "no savvy" that. They don't understand that. Finally we tried our delegation out there, our congressional delegation, but they don't do a darn thing either. As I say, we don't have old-time Alaskans like we used to have.

Now if we had a guy out there with guts like old Bob Bartlett, he'd get things done.[23] That's one of the old-time Alaskans. These other ones are the Johnny-come-latelys. I don't classify them with the old-time Alaskans. They are a different breed of people.

Yup, Bob Bartlett, he'd get things done. Like after the war, we had trouble there. The boys were discharged and then they kicked them out, you know. Well we went after Bob Bartlett and he put a stop to that right away. He saw to it that the boys were sent back to their homes, that they had enough money to get back home, yeah. I don't know what in the world they done that to us for, I don't know. But anyway, Bob Bartlett said, "Anything like that happen again, you boys let me know." And as I say, he's one of those real old-time Alaskans that gets things done, yeah.

Anyway, the plan was that I was to go to school out in the States. But, as always, money was short. When I worked for the railroad, why we saved all that money. I worked four different seasons for the railroad and we saved that money, and the money I made from extra work with the dogs, like when I worked for Deputy Marshal Hagen and Mr.

"That's the Miller family, Maynard, Bub, and Mrs. Miller.
They're the ones that took me in, treated me just like one of their
boys. If it wasn't for them, I don't think I would have made it."

Senafe. Oh, they paid good, them fellows. Well that money went towards my schooling. So I was able to go out on the new Alaska Railroad.[24] And then, from Anchorage we got on a boat and went down. And then we travelled across the States down there on the railroad. Finally wound up at Mt. Hermon, in Mt. Hermon, Massachusetts. And then I went to school there for three years and towards the last there, I had to work as a working student because the money was low. You know, you work all day and then you take a couple of classes.

I believe that I would have never made it out there if it wasn't for getting acquainted with the Miller family. The Miller family had a farm in Vermont, in Vernon, Vermont. They had a modern farm and they were sending their son to Mt. Hermon School. That's how I got acquainted with him. He took me home with him and they just took me in as one of their boys and they treated me as one of their boys. And if it wasn't for them, I don't believe I would have lasted a year out there. So, I really have much to thank those people for, the Miller family.

And I understand that one of the boys is still out there. And one of them got into politics and he was the congressman I think for Vermont there. Miller was his name.

We didn't have money to come back to Alaska in summer. It's pretty slow going when you have to work and you get paid fifteen cents an hour. That's what we used to get.

Well, I stayed out there for three years. I finally got homesick for Alaska and then finally made my way back, back home to Alaska, yes. And then that was the time I started working under Mr. Nicholson, that master mechanic that put up all these mission buildings. And I work under him for seven years, travelling all over, and putting up these mission buildings. I worked under him, and he had that old boat, the *Pelican*, that was a work boat. It shoved two, three barges, hauling our sawmill equipment and tools and stuff like that. And Mr. Nicholson, he had a couple of real carpenters, you know, real trained carpenters along. And then he had two, three young Native kids like me and Jimmy Bruce and Archie Moses. We were along to learn. Jimmy Bruce, he was a first class mechanic. He's just like Clinton Wiehl, you know. Those old fellows catch on naturally. But me, I'm pretty slow except for that sawmill work, I like that sawmill work. And that is where I learned to oper-

"That's the working Pelican. *Archie Moses is in the cabin. He's the cook. And Jimmy Bruce is on deck. He's part of the building crew."*

ate a small sawmill, from Mr. Nicholson. We travelled up and down the Yukon to different places, and we put up new buildings, log buildings.

Mr. Nicholson had a portable sawmill and everywhere we went, they used to build mission stations. We had to go out and we had to do our own logging. We had to get our own logs, cut them up and build the building. And Mr. Nicholson saw that I was interested in the sawmill, so he did his best to show me how to cut lumber. Oh, he was strict as could be, I remember. And if I made a little mistake, why he jumped up and down. But he was good. Everything had to be just so. And well, he's so doggone strict that I don't think in all that time we even put a burned spot on the saw. All our saws, we got them and operated them so that they worked cool. And I found out that's one of the things you have to be watchful about is not to burn your saw. You know, you can ruin your saw in no time. But we didn't even have a burned spot on our saw, he was so strict. Anyway, what little I did know about sawing I learned from him. And towards the last, he let me do the sawing. Oh, he was there to watch. So, in that way, I learned how to operate the small sawmill.

And we went from place to place, to these different mission stations, and we did everything to put up these buildings. This is over a series of years. We did work at Nenana. We put up a big building. We even came here to Fairbanks, to St. Mathew's Mission, and we put in a new foundation on that old church, yes. And we went to Tanana, and we went up to Fort Yukon. We did a lot of work up there. When we came back down, we went all the way up to Allakaket. We put up buildings there. This is over a number of years. It took a number of years to put in new buildings at all these places. But he was a hard taskmaster, Mr. Nicholson. Everything had to be just so, you know.

One year I was still working for the church and we came in from a short trip out on the trail, came in before Christmas, back to Nenana before Christmas. And they wanted a teacher down at Minto. The teacher that was supposed to come in didn't show up for some reason. They wanted me to try to help out down there as a teacher. The regular teacher there at St. Mark's Mission, she gave me a lot of instructions on how to start teaching the children ABC's and stuff like that. And besides reading, writing and a little arithmetic, we have to study the Bible too, since that was a church school.

"The first time I was working for Mr. Nicholson we put in a new foundation on this church."

"I think that this is the one we worked on at Allakaket."

So, I took the dogs down. We didn't have much equipment. All we had was a box full of scrap writing paper, a handful of used pencils, and a piece of blackboard material and half a box of chalk. I had my grub and my trail gear: snowshoes, rifle, axe, stuff like that. And I took off for Minto, got down there and here was the building already put up, a little cabin and the school house. People had wood cut there. They knew that I was coming. Them days there was that telegraph system and people heard that I was coming so the place was all warm.

So we started school right the next day. And I filled in there as substitute teacher for a couple of years. Of course, the people down Minto now have moved to the new area, what they call the New Minto. But those days we used to go over in the area of New Minto to hunt caribou, over the weekend. The caribou was all over those days and it didn't take us long to get what we need and get back, get back to Old Minto before the weekend is over so we'd be ready to start school again on Monday. And then, besides teaching school, we had to have church services and instructions in the Bible. There was some people down there at Minto that took part in a lot of the teaching in the church. The people would come there and hold service and then they would have Sunday school. A lot of that work was done by the people themselves. I was there for a couple of seasons, yes.

IN SEARCH OF GOLD

After I got through working for the church and after I was out on my own, I was travelling out in the country with Chief Christian and his family. Here's the way it started. Mr. Rodman was the NC manager at Fort Yukon at the time, and it seems like somebody came in and showed him a handful of nuggets, somebody from the Christian outfit, yeah. Oh, he was all excited then. And there was an old-timer there by the name of Mr. Leonard Lord, he was cutting steamboat wood, and he's one of the old-timers who knew all about prospecting. So Mr. Rodman grubstaked him. He said, "I'll give you everything you need, but you've got to have somebody to go with you. You pick out some young person."

He was a man long in years, but he could still get along pretty good. So they picked me. I was out on my own then. I spent quite a number of years with Mr. Leonard Lord and I learned what little I know about prospecting from him. He's one of the old-timers who came into the country in the early days.

Well, as I said, Mr. Leonard Lord and Chief Christian and Mr. Rodman, they're all, well, just like partners on this prospecting deal. We went out there with a dog team and we used the dogs for sledding when we have snow, and then we use them as pack dogs. We stayed out there a summer and we did a lot of travelling around, testing here and there, hundreds of creeks up there. And one place we had our cache. We made a great big cache when the caribou were there in the fall, you know. And the caribou were real fat, in good shape. We dried some of that meat and we put it in this cache and then we took off, way up on Smoke Creek. We were gone for about a month or so and then we came back. We camped about two miles away from the cache and Chief Christian sent one of the boys down, one of the kids, to see how the cache was. He was only about ten years old. And he told him, "If you see any bear

69

around, keep away."

So this kid, he went there and here was a great big old bear. And the doggone kid, I don't know what the heck, he was foolish I guess. Anyway, he shot. He had a .44, you know, .44 Winchester. He sneaked up close in the timber area and he fired. He shot that bear right in the left hand. And then the bear started roaring and tearing up all the vegetation there. While he's doing that the kid, he took off, beat it back to camp. Lucky he got back to camp.

So next day we went there, Chief Christian, this boy, and myself. And here was this bear. There's a creek there, you know, and the bear was laying right in the creek. I was going to go up there. I thought he was dead, you know. I go up there and Chief Christian hollered just in time, "Get back here." I backed up a ways and just then that bear got up. And oh, he was a monster. And then, right then Chief Christian, he's working his rifle. He had a 30-40 Model 1895. That was his favorite rifle too. He was working that thing like a machine gun, and I was so surprised I just stood there and didn't even fire. And the kid with his .44, he had that working full blast too. Me, I was so surprised. I just stood there and did nothing until Chief Christian hollered at me, "Shoot!" By then the bear was standing up. That's the time I come to. Then I fired. I had a 30-06, a bolt action 30-06 Winchester. I come to and hit him in a vital place and then, of course, he come down. He was a big monster that bear, one of the biggest bears that I ever seen in my life, and I've seen a good many of them. He was a monster.

Later on, two or three years later on, when our prospecting never turned out, that is, we never found no pay, then I contracted with Mr. Ambro. Mr. Ambro came into the country in 1896. I spent a number of years with him, and I learned quite a lot from him too. Mr. William Ambro was one of the early-day locators there on Big Creek. There was pay there, but he's one of those guys, he can't stay in one place, you know, he has got to keep going. There was good pay on that creek but he left there and he wanted to go somewhere else, looking for something better, I guess. See he and Mr. Mello were partners. They come into the country together in 1896.

Anyway, for years and years after that he had to go back to the Yukon River and make a grubstake by cutting steamboat wood. Of course steamboat wood was in big demand those days. Mr. Ambro, he would cut and yard anywhere from 150 to 200 cords of steamboat wood, cut it and haul it with dogs to the bank of the Yukon there. And then he has enough grubstake there for two or three years, yeah. That's the way he used to make his grubstake. I learned about prospecting from him. He was on a trip up the Chandalar and he wanted me to go with him so I did. That's where I learned from him. We did a lot of work together up there. We sunk a lot of holes all over, and we built cabins on the North Fork of the East Fork. We sunk a lot of holes there. To get up there, we would line and pole them days. We didn't have no engines like they have now—line and pole.[25] We had our dogs and we haul up to the North Fork of the East Fork they call that. And we built our cabin there. We got our cabin up before the cold, and then we got in our supply of wood, caribou, and everything. And it was in there that Ambro had a cache.

He couldn't locate that cache. While he was trying to locate that cache, I was sinking holes. We were sinking holes you see. We just use wood fire. That's awfully slow work, you know. It was a wood fire for thawing out. After we get fire going I'd just watch it, while he'd go out looking for his cache. He'd come back and, "No, nope. It must be wrong place." Well, one time I says, I told him, "You watch the fire, I'll go out and take a look."

So I took off and went up, I forget how many miles. I went up about four miles I think, up river from there, where there's a creek come in. You look in there, why it's just a dead end. But you go in a ways and it makes a right angle. That's where it deceives you if you look from the river see. It looks like no creek there. So, I follow that creek and here it open up into a wide valley, and then I see a big cache standing up there. So I went up there, I was snowshoeing. And by golly, here was an old-fashioned boiler underneath that cache, and all kinds of stuff on top of that cache. So I went up there.

Ambro was short of tobacco and Johnny Frank was supposed to come up from Venetie with a load, but he hadn't showed up yet. Well, I look in this cache, there's all kinds of stuff in that cache, grub from way back. He cached it there years ago, you know. The tobacco was still good, it was in tin cans—"Edgeworth."

71

Well I took one of those cans, stuck it in my packsack, and I went back to camp. Here he was sawing wood out there. Well I told him, "I found your cache." He said, "No, you didn't find my cache." I said, "Sure, look at here." I gave him his can of tobacco. Well, the first thing he did was to fill up his pipe. After we had tea, then we hook up dogs and went out there. It's not too far from there. Sure enough that's his cache, that's the one he built there years ago, yeah. And some of that stuff was still good there. Tobacco was still good, and the boiler, of course the boiler was still good. And we used that old boiler there to sink holes.

We sunk holes there and then later on we moved down to, well, they named that place where we prospected, they called it Gold Camp afterwards. Johnny Frank named it Gold Camp.

Later on Johnny Frank kept talking to Ambro about that creek down there. So before too late, we moved down to this place. And Johnny Frank already started a cabin for us there, so we finished it. It didn't take us long to finish the cabin. And then we sunk two or three holes on that creek with our boiler there. We found gold there too but it's flour gold, you know. It's got a lot of work to be done in order to find out for sure whether or not there's any pay in it. Anyway, Johnny Frank settled in that area and that's the one they call Gold Creek.

And then later on when I was on my own, I did a lot of other prospecting way in the Interior. I've got two, three boilers scattered all over the Interior here. I got a boiler over here at Heart Mountain, and I got a boiler over here at that camp, that Gold Creek. Then I had another boiler up above Hardpac. I did a lot of work on Hardpac but I never found a darn thing. Then I moved it to Slate Creek. I moved in there and that boiler, that outfit, my prospecting outfit, I left there. And then an outfit come into the Koyukuk and took the whole darn works, you know.[26]

I spent one season over at the head of Black River. My uncle, Paul Henry, his trapline is up there. He got me up there one year. He paid all the expenses. He want me to sink some holes there or do some panning. And then I spent time over in the Koyukuk and I spent a lot of time up in the Hodzana. Yes, I've gone all over the Interior there. I've practically prospected all over, yeah.

I travelled around winter and summer. And summertime we had our dogs, they carried packs. Packs. You have to see that pack is the correct size and then you load it properly so that it doesn't hurt the dog. You have to be awfully careful of that. Some of those prospectors, they made pack out of canvas, you know, and they made them too big. And when you load them, they're way down on the dog, and they rubbed down on their legs. Now, that's not very good. But those Native-made ones, those Native-made ones, are made out of caribou leg skins, you know. Every time they get a caribou leg they save the skin. It's tanned and put to one side for later use. And these Native-made dog packs are made out of these tanned caribou leg skins. Oh yeah, they're nice strong packs. Well-built. And then they rode high on the dogs. But you had to have a pack strap on there to tie it down. They have a strap about eight or ten feet long and it's about an inch and a half, two inches wide, and after you get the pack on the dog, you tie it down with this certain hitch. That way the pack will stay on the top of the dog. If it's an old pack dog you can put quite a bit of load on him. But breaking in a pack dog you had to be awful careful not to put in too big of a load at the start, you know. You put a pack on a dog for the first time, why he'll buck just like a horse. He can't get it off then he'll roll around all over and oh, he'll have a heck of a time, but he'll learn. He'll learn. After he learns, he'll learn to take care of that pack. Yes. He won't go in where there's water until you tell him to. Sometime you come to a creek, it's too deep, you know, and you have to take the packs off and you pack it across yourself. The dogs come across and you put them on again on the other side. But they won't go in a creek while they got that load on. They know, those dogs. Yeah.

I remember some of the early, old-time Native prospectors. Oh, there are quite a lot of them, but just these few that I remember: Sam Pingalo is one of them, and Sam Hope, and Turak Newman. Turak Newman is one of the best of them, yeah. And then, of course, there's some of those real old-timers, the Pitkas, and the Mynooks. Those guys made big discoveries.

Well, so far as Mynook and Pitka, I never did meet them but I heard stories and everything. They were the ones that first discovered gold up in that Hodzana country, up in there. They travelled around. They were

73

great prospectors those two guys, you know. They just lived off the country. As long as they had a good rifle and enough ammunition and fish hooks, they got along. They lived practically off the country and then they did a lot of mining down around Rampart area too, so I understand. They were the first ones down in there.[27]

Of course, those Natives that discovered that gold up in Dawson, Skookum Jim and Tagish Charlie, you know, there's a lot of different stories about who made that discovery up there. And according to the Natives, it's those guys, Skookum Jim and Tagish Charlie. They knew about where that gold was all the time, yeah. They were the regular discoverers of that place. I understand their brother-in-law left them after they hit the pay and even deserted his wife and all that, married another White woman after he made all that big money. But the real discoverers, according to the Natives, were those two guys, Tagish Charlie and Skookum Jim. That's the Native version of it.

MINING WORK IN FAIRBANKS

Well, to go prospecting you've got to have money. You've got to have an outfit and supplies. And the only place where we can make a grub-stake those days, besides cutting steamboat wood, was coming over here to Fairbanks. There's a lot of mining going on around this area those days. There was drift mines and there were dredges. I started working, I remember, out there at Livengood. There was a dredge there that I worked on. I worked on that dredge for two seasons and then later on, in other years, I came over and I worked for the FE; I worked on their dredge one year and then a couple of years I work as what they call a pipe walker.[28] Anybody that knows anything about those days, they know what a pipe walker is. My job was to walk the line and see that everything is in order and patch here and there as I go along.

And then after that I came back and I worked out in a drift mine, out there at Chatanika for Olley, Locke, Blake, and Larson. They're old-timers in the country and they had a lay on that ground there, deep underground mining. And the First National Bank had interest in there too, in that mine. Everytime we had a cleanup I remember they send one of their representatives out there. I used to come over there every year for quite a number of years, working in that drift mine. And we worked in the drift there with a gang of men, pick and shovel and wheelbarrow.

That's down in the drift, drift mine. Right down you go, right down probably 125-30 feet and then you go in there and work in the dirt. You work in a gang of men, probably about ten men, maybe twelve men, all depending on what size bucket you got there, twelve-wheelbarrow or ten-wheelbarrow or whatever. And then you had to keep your place in the line. The leader of this gang, he's a great big powerful six-and-a-half-foot Russian, shoulders on him about two axe handles wide. He sets the pace and he gets a dollar a day extra for it. And the rest of us guys have to keep up with him, and if we don't keep up with him we get fired. Anyway, we work. We really had to work them days, yup.

Well, this particular place was awfully rich ground there and they had a cleanup every ten days, yeah. And that was quite a time. The boys all celebrated. And the owners, they furnished all the booze they wanted to drink and everything. Those were the days when booze was hitting the market again. Oh, they had a wild time, cleanup time.

Well, the first time, I remember they had all that wine, beer, and whiskey. I was still with my partner, Albert Fleishman. You've heard of him, a lot of old-timers remember him, yeah. Oh, he was a boozer, you know. He's way older than I was. And I was sitting and watching. Pretty soon the old-timer, he's from the old country, I think he was an Austrian. Oh boy, did he give me a talking too. He says, "You leave those drinks alone. Leave the drink alone. It's just going to ruin you. Let them fellas go. You can't tell them guys nothing. But you, you are a young man; you leave that alone. I'm just telling you what it will do. It will ruin you. You'll be no doggone good if you go to that stuff. I tell you, it's up to you. If you want to, go ahead. But I tell you not to."

And I forgot that man's name, but he was an old-timer. Boy, did he give me the works, yeah. So I didn't touch a doggone thing, yeah. All that time, I didn't touch a doggone thing. And he was right too. That old-timer was right. He knew what he was talking about, yeah, He gave me the facts of life—about booze.

Another man I remember from Fairbanks was Mr. McPhee. I met him when I first came over to Fairbanks looking for work, and he's a World War I marine. And he's a gun nut from way back, a gun crank, you know. I met him and he was working in the office there at the railroad, so in that way I got to know him. And everytime I came to Fairbanks area, why I stayed with him. And then, as I said, later on when he started building these new loads of ammunition, why I tried them out on game. Mr. McPhee did a lot of hand loading, you know. He was working with Mr. Elmer Keith. I believe he was the one that developed the magnum hand guns, cartridges. And they furnished me with Smith and Wessons, you know, and then Mr. McPhee, why he hand loaded the ammunition. I had all modern hand guns. Oh boy, they're dandy shooting guns, lot of power there. And then I had to tell at what distance I fired the shot, and where I hit and how far it penetrated and all that. They were powerful guns those magnum guns and I generally got right up close and generally one shot did the work, yeah. The first one we worked on was that 357 magnum I think, yes, 357 magnum. And I tested it out on game and I sent in my report to them. That 357 is a wonderful handgun. At close range it will knock over any game that walks, if you place the bullet properly.

And then we just got through with the 357 and we start in on the 41 and the 44 magnum. They'll work, if you place your bullet right. And as I say, those hand guns are close range weapons and you should never try to let them do the work of a rifle. They're a close range weapon and if you place your bullet right, those magnum handguns will deliver.

I also remember Billy Root from Fairbanks. A lot of the old-timers remember him. He used to operate sort of a freighting service out to the creeks. And he used to come out there every second or third day, out to where I was working, out there at Chatanika.

And another person that I used to know, who was there at that time, was Sam Estus. He ran a store out there at Chatanika, Sam Estus. And Pat, Pat ran a store out there, Patton. I got acquainted with him. And of course, you'll never forget old Two Step Louie. He was out there too. He was living in a cabin out there.

I remember one time we just got out of the hole, you know, and we were on our way to the bunkhouse and cookhouse, just a little ways away from where we were working. And we run into old Two Step and he had a nice train of fish, grayling. The boys wanted to know where in the world he got them. He said you got to be a good fisherman like him or you don't catch them. He said, "Oh, there's lots of them, but you got to know how to catch them."

Well, anyway, the outcome was that all the boys said they got to go fishing after supper. So after supper two truck loads left the camp and went towards town. The road went out by town. And we're supposed to turn left, but after they got to town, they turned to the right. They hollered, "What they going to do?" Oh, they said they going to have one drink of beer before they go fishing. Well, anyway, the outcome was that they drank every bit of beer that Sam Estus had in his store there and then they went up to Mr. Patton's store. Mr. Patton and his wife Helen, they had a store there. But they were closed. So they came all the way to Fox and they cleaned up everything they had there at Fox and we got back to camp just in time to go to work. So, that was quite a fishing trip we had there.

And then another man out there was Julius Stolsus, the mining foreman. I think he was an Austrian. I remember him real well because he was interested in the Native people, you know. And any Native people coming here to look for work, he went out of his way to see that they got jobs. He was really quite a help. Not only me, he helped a lot of other Natives looking for work in those days, you know. Julius always had a few dollars to help out. He saw that I was interested in prospecting. And then in the evening when we got through work, he would tell me what to do, like coming to a creek and panning and all that stuff about prospecting. I learned lots from him.

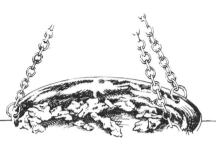

BACK TO THE CREEKS

We saved that money and we got supplies to go out prospecting. Yup, we would save our money, and I would go back to Beaver. And Frank Yasuda, the storekeeper there, he'd have my stuff, outfit for me, and I'd spend another year out in the hills prospecting. Oh, I had some partners. I prospected with different men. One of the men that I prospected with was Harry Francis. He's still mining. He's in his eighties I think, but he's still mining, yes. He's a good man out in the woods. Harry Francis was one of the best. We lived off the country together, him and me.

But this one year my uncle Paul Henry sent for me. He thought there was gold up by his camp, but he don't want to take a pan. "Oh yeah, I'm no prospector." That's what he used to say. But he wanted me to come up there and he's going to pay all my expenses. Anyway, I went up to Fort Yukon. He tell me, "Get anything you want."

Well, I just come from the hills, you know. I need some new overalls, a shirt, stuff like that. That way he ordered me anything I wanted there. And then we took off. In a couple, three days we were up at his place. He had the trapping country way up at the head of the Porcupine River, and that's supposed to be one of the best trapping areas in the country. And he had the reputation of being quite a hustler; he didn't waste time. He liked to come to town, yes, like around Christmas time he'd come in and then join in the festivities, you know. He'd join in and have a good time. But when it's time to work, he's out there, right there, right on the dot. And he made wonderful catches, big catches. And he would come down in the spring after break-up.[29] Of course, he got married as soon as he was old enough to get married and he has his family with him. In the early days they use poling boats. Later on, when the motors came, why he had one of the best rigs in the country.

There was an old-timer in Fort Yukon, he made his living making boats and putting in engines for these trappers. And one of the first boats that he rigged up was the one for my uncle, Paul Henry. I remember that boat, it's an inboard, you know, Gray motor I think, Gray Marine Motor, yeah something like that. Anyway, he had one of the best there. He had that rig for years and years. Every spring he'd come down. He had a barge with it too, you know, loaded down with all his fur and dogs, and his wife and kids and everything, coming into Fort Yukon. And then they would stay at Fort Yukon. He would sell his fur. Oh, he would be loaded down with furs. In those days, the trading posts had almost anything that you can think of. This is after my grandfather's days, after the steamboat started running regularly. And those trading posts, they had everything. Not like now. You go to some of those villages now and there's hardly nothing in the store. Not those days, those steamboat days. Those trading posts had everything you can think of: hams, bacon, and all kinds of canned stuff, and dried stuff, put up properly too, in small cans, you know, five and ten pound boxes.

You don't see anything like that nowadays. Those days trappers were outfitted real good and they had quite a variety of food, including fruits, dried fruits, all kinds, prunes, and dried apples and peaches and stuff like that, besides all the other stuff.

And my uncle, in the fall he starts out loaded down, barge and boat loaded down with his winter's outfit. But his barge was big enough so that he could handle it all. He'd get back to his trapline, back to his cabin on the Porcupine in time to rustle wood for the family. All that's got to be done. And then hunting too, you know, hunting for the winter meat, that's got to be done before freeze-up. Lot of work to be done out in the camp, in the trapper camp. He had quite a place up there.

Oh, he had a dandy place there. It's a two-story building. He's a man that is particular, you know. Everything had to be just so. He's one of those guys that's just a natural born carpenter I guess. He never went to school for carpenter work, or anything like that. But he can build a sled or snowshoes or build a cabin without any mistakes. Anyway, he had a wonderful place there. There was everything inside the kitchen part. He had one of those big cast iron cook stoves there. He brought it in with the boat during the summer. And he had a big heater there. And then upstairs there's different rooms there for men and for women too. Everything had to be in its place. And he is a particular man, as I say. You know, before you eat, you have to wash. He had a place to wash there and all that.

Anyway he got me up there. He said, "Now over there on that creek, I want you to sink some holes over there, or pan or whatever you have to do. I think there's gold there." So, I went over there. There's exposed bedrock, so all I had to do was build campfires, two or three campfires, and thaw right there on bedrock and I can pan right there. Thaw out and melt water and pan right there. I raised gold there. Oh, there's good prospects up in this part of the country, yeah. And I told him, there's gold there, and I showed him these other minerals. I told him there's all kinds of minerals there. Well, that's what he wanted to know. So I stayed there that winter with him and he told me, "Now we found out. If you want to trap out that way, run a line out that way." So I spent the rest of this winter doing a little trapping there. I trapped for marten too. He gave me all the traps I wanted whenever I wanted it. Oh, he was on his long lines, you know, and he'd be gone for three or four days all this time.

There were a lot of wolves in that country and I went out and hunted wolves. I caught three in the snare and then I shot four. One time I happened to come out on a lake, and oh, a lot of caribou coming through there. Well, I was coming by there and a cow was just on the edge of that lake. I hadn't gotten out on the lake yet. I look up there, and by golly here comes four wolves, four black wolves, yeah. So I got right down in the brush there and I waited. I waited until they got right in the center of the lake and then I opened up on them. I got all four. After the first shot, of course, they took off pretty fast, but they were fairly close so I was able to get them all.

Well, I came in after break-up in the spring. You know, that's when he come in with his boat. So I came back to Beaver and I went back to my prospecting.

Another partner you've heard me mention was Ambro, William Ambro. He's one of the real old-timers that came into the country in 1896. He came in by way of the Kogruak. He came into the Interior and he spent all his time out prospecting. One year, I was with him helping to

81

prospect and doing all the work necessary that goes with prospecting. And it was time to come back and earn another grubstake. We used up all our food and supplies and we had to get back and earn some more money so we could go prospecting again. He came back to Beaver and started cutting steamboat wood. By the time spring came along, why he had over a hundred and fifty cords of wood, steamboat wood, cut and stacked right on the riverbank there.

And me, I went trapping with my brother-in-law, Solomon Adams. He was a partially disabled man but he was a good honest man and good hard worker and he was married to my sister. Mr. Ambro told me, he said, "Moses, your brother-in-law's down there and he's a semi-invalid, but he's a good hard working man. Your brother needs you. You better move down to Beaver and help him run that trapline." So I pitched in and helped him. He had one of the best traplines in the country. I helped him, and we built a lot of new cabins; we cut out a lot of new lines and we made a good going proposition out of it.

Now trapping in those days was a year around proposition. During the summer, after break-up, I would help my brother-in-law and my sister to get their fish camp up. I helped them put up their fish wheels, fix up the fish camps, fish racks, and move all the dogs there. Then after that, while they handled that all summer, I would take off and I'd head up the Hodzana. I'd spend the whole summer way up in the woods there prospecting on my own. In those days, I had a little homemade wooden boat. We didn't have these nice big aluminum boats like they have nowadays. And I had two of those old fashioned two and a half horsepower Johnson outboard motors, with heavy duty three prong propellers. You can't wear those things out. They go slow but you get there. I never had any trouble with them darn things, not like the ones we have now. They're just made to give you trouble!

Well, anyway, I would spend my whole summer way up there. Besides prospecting, I would stop at the different trapline cabins and I would cut a bunch of wood and pack it into the cabin there. Oh, we had so many trapline cabins. It kept me busy all summer just to have enough wood, enough wood to at least get started in the trapping season. And then I did some prospecting too; I prospected for years up there. I found gold but not what you would call real pay. I'd come back down towards fall.

By that time, my brother-in-law and my sister, they would have a boat-load of dried fish for me to take up to our headquarters cabin. So, I'd load up with that baled fish. They used to be standard size fifty pound bales those days. And that was just as good as gold those dog team days.[30] So, I took a load up to headquarters cabin, up the Hodzana. That's a two or three day trip one way. Sometimes I had to make three trips because besides baled fish, we had to take up our grub too, for the winter. So, sometimes I made three trips. That kept me pretty busy.

And then before freeze-up there, towards fall the main thing is to get in some meat for the family. In those days that was very easy because there was a lot of game in the country. So before freeze-up, or just during freeze-up, we'd get what moose we'd need for the family.

In later years the family have to stay in town there so the kids can go to school. And then, after we can travel with the dogs, then we take off. We take off for our traplines, light load—we're not loaded down. And then we get up to our headquarters cabin and by that time trapping season is started and we go right to work trapping. We extend our lines from what we call our headquarters cabin. From there we had lines north, lines all directions, cabins here and there. And most of my job was looking after lines. But my brother-in-law, he look after his lines that's closest to the headquarters cabin. I took care of all the far away lines. And he stuck around the headquarters cabin as he did most of the skinning. I would bring in most of the fur, like lynx and marten and stuff like that. I would come in with a sled load of frozen fur for him to skin out. I leave it there and the next day I take off and cover a lot of ground. And, of course, out on the trapline, once in a while I run across fur that's freshly caught. While it's still fresh, I skin it out myself. But most of my time, why I picked up fur and then gathered them up and brought them to headquarters cabin. That kept me pretty busy. And my brother-in-law, he spent most of his time there skinning out and drying. He did a lot of running around from there with his own dog team. I had my own dog team too. So, we covered a lot of ground. I remember one creek up at the foot of Dall Mountain there. I could name that one creek Lynx Creek. Oh, my golly, I used to go down there and I would come back trying to pack four or five of those lynx stretched out and frozen all kind of directions. How I used to cuss them. We only got about five and a half or seven dollars apiece for them, them days. We caught a lot of fur but we didn't get very high prices for them. But we made a good living.

And another thing, you know my brother-in-law, he used skis. He learned that skiing from an old Norwegian there. Einer Hagen was his name. He's one of the real old-timers who came into the country, I don't know when. Anyway, he's no prospector; he's a trapper, trapper from way back. He used skis, and he taught my brother-in-law how to use skis. He knew my brother-in-law when he was just a kid. And he taught him how to use skis. And when I started trapping with my brother-in-law he wanted me to use skis. Well, after I fell on my backside a couple of times, why I switched back to snowshoes. Anyway, my brother-in-law, he used skis and he covers more ground than I do with the snowshoes because with the skis you can go much faster than with snowshoes.

This old-timer made those skis by himself and then later on my brother-in-law made skis. He learned from Mr. Hagen how to make these short, wide skis, you know. And then they were treated on the bottom with some kind of a mixture. I don't know. I'm no ski man, but they fix something on the bottom and that help it slide. They sure cover a lot of ground.

Well, anyway we would come in at Christmas time to Beaver and stay for the celebration, Christmas and New Year. In those days all the trappers came in and that's before booze and whiskey ruined the villages. And the people used to have a real good time, wonderful time. They dance all night long and then they have a community hall there where everybody pitch in and cook. Everybody pitched in and did their share of work. Everybody just having one heck of a good time. That goes on for about two weeks and then they have to go back in the woods again trapping after Christmas, yes.

Then we went right back out after New Year's. And we didn't come back in until after the trapping season is over. We would get through there and then beaver season is open. So we get busy on that. I remember those early days there's no limit on beaver. We got quite a few beaver because we were right in the beaver country there.

We would come to town before muskrat hunting and get what little stuff we need and then go back out again and hunt muskrats. We trap them through the ice and then later on, after lakes are open, then we go around with canoes; we shoot them. We shoot them with 22's. We would dry those muskrats. Those good fat ones, you cut them up right to dry. Oh, they're good eating. The same way with the beaver too. You cut them up just right so they'll dry. By golly, you talk about good eating. They'll keep for quite a while too, you know. That way you have something to fall back on to eat. It's awfully rich meat, yeah. So we spent the spring there, right out there on the trapline, trapping muskrats, shooting muskrats, and shooting beaver.

We caught quite a bit of fur compared to what they're doing nowadays, yeah. We caught a lot of fur them days. But, of course, the prices are not like they are now, you know.

And then, by that time the ducks will be coming in too, you know. And, of course, I know it's against the law now, but those days we killed ducks to eat, what we needed to eat.

We were never short of anything. We had everything we needed. The supplies came all the way from out in the States,[31] yes. And that's way before airplane days and stuff like that. Oh, we had everything good those days. A little bit slow in getting there but when it got there, it was something you could depend on, yeah. And it seems like in those days everything was put up different from the way they are nowadays. Everything was put up to keep—wooden boxes and stuff like that. And everything came first-class shape. Everything is good—good bacon and stuff like that. They even used to have dog bacon and dog rice. Dog rice is cheaper than the other, you know. And it seems like those days everything seems to be of better quality too.

We traded with Frank Yasuda and he used to have barge loads of supplies come there. He had a couple of big warehouses just loaded down. And then, when he outfit you, he see that you got the best. Anything that is a little bit spoiled or a little bit old he'd throw away. That's the kind of trader Frank Yasuda was. He gives you nothing but the best and plenty of it. And Frank, he trusted everybody, practically everybody he trusted. And I know he didn't lose any money on me and my brother-in-law, but I think he trusted maybe too many guys. A lot of guys were not able to pay, you know. And that way he must of lost a few dollars too. But he never turned a person down, Frank Yasuda. And as I said, the stuff he got those days had to be first-class quality or else he threw it away, yeah.

PAY DIRT

In the fall of 1941, getting toward freeze-up, I was taking a load of dry fish up to our home cabin. Well, this particular trip, I started kind of late in the afternoon and I had to camp that night up on the Hodzana. I know where there's a good place to camp so I camp there. After I had something to eat, I went down to the boat, and by golly, this sediment look kind of funny. So I had a gold pan and shovel right there. I grabbed the shovel and tried to get a shovel full of that. I can't make a dent in it. So I got my pick and I picked it loose. And you hit it just right, it crumbles, you know. By golly, I got a pan full of that, and just as soon as I laid my hands on that gold pan and put it in the water, I knew there was something different.

Of all the pans I've ever taken, I believe that is the richest pan that I ever took. After I pan it way down, oh, the black sand on it was that thick, you know. I panned it down on a big standard size gold pan, and on the rim of the pan for about ten, twelve inches, there it's just yellow, like corn meal, you know. Flour gold.

Oh, I got all excited. I thought well, by golly, I finally hit it. And I made out what in the world was I going to do. Shall I stake now or no? Well, I decided no; I better not stake now because it's too late in the season. But next spring, I'll come up right after break-up and stake and take out some of this here flour gold. I was going to raise Cain that next year.

I found out that I was selfish too, you know. I say if I stake now, all these guys going to come and they're going to stake around. So I said I'm going to wait till next spring, in the spring of 1942. I'm going to wait, and then I'm going to stake and I'm going to record it before I let anybody know. Oh boy, I had big plans, I was going to raise Cain.

By golly, I took this load up to our home cabin and then I went back and made another trip and then I got all our stuff up to the home cabin. Then, after it was cold enough, we started out with our dog teams from Beaver. We started out on our regular trapping and at Christmas time, that's when we found out our country was tangled up with the war. When we came back to Beaver for the Christmas holidays, that's the time I found this draft card there, draft notice. So I had to report to Fairbanks. That's where I was told to report.

And when I finally got back to that place on the Hodzana, there was ten feet of muck covering the whole doggone place. The river raises Cain, you know. It moves dirt, everything on top of it. Why a poor man like me can't do nothing unless he's got a million dollars of equipment to get in there. So I lost that one big chance that I had.

"We usually put in a long day travelling; then we pitch camp and have a good supper. I usually do the cooking."

SERVING UNCLE SAM
AND MORE PROSPECTING

Well, in them days you either had to go over and report for duty or else go to jail. I didn't want to go to jail so I came over. And when I got over here I reported out at Ladd Field. There was a great big gang of Alaskans—Indians, Eskimos, White boys, Aleuts, a whole bunch of them. They been piling in out there, every plane bringing them in. There's a whole bunch of them there and I was told that I had to take them down to Anchorage. I was in charge. I had a little military service before and on account of that they put me in charge. "Well," I thought to myself, "how in the world am I going to take care of that wild bunch?"

We went down there on the train. Oh, I had quite a time there, you can imagine. Over a hundred head of them to look after. Well, anyway, I didn't have much trouble with them. They were OK. They did a lot of drinking, made a lot of noise, but they were OK. Finally, I got them down to Anchorage, got them down there safe and sound and then we reported in there.

That's where all the Alaskans were coming in, coming in all day and night. Oh, lots of them coming in there. And that night, after I was on the go I don't know how many hours, I thought I was going to hit the sack. Here comes a fellow coming down the street, Company Street there, hollering my name. So I stuck my head out and said, "Here I am." He came in and he said, "You Moses Cruikshank?" I said, "Yeah." "Here," he said, "take a drink." I told him, "I don't drink." He said, "Ok, that's good. You're from Beaver up in the Hodzana? You know anything about the Hodzana country?" I said, "Yes, I trap up in there." He said, "Listen are you interested in prospecting?" I said, "Sure, I done a lot of that, but I never found anything that pay yet." "Well," he said, "I have information here. If we come out of this alive,

I want you and me to go back up in the Hodzana and we'll have her made." "Well, by golly," I said, "I've never found nothing yet." "Well," he said, "listen to me." Then he told me the story about this young man. Oh, he was working for some publishing outfit, it looks like old history, something like that, and he run across the records, those old steamboat records up there in, where was it, Dawson or Eagle, or someplace around there? Anyway he said, "It's in the books where this same young man—first thing he did in the summer was to get off the boat at the mouth of the Hodzana and then in the fall he get on one of those last boats going out. Everything is kept record of. The purser, he kept track of everything. Anyway, one of the first things he did was put his poke of gold with the purser, you know.[32] It was a good size poke, yeah. This went on for three or four years. And someplace up there, there's a good place for gold."

I said, "By golly that's the first time I ever hear of it, but I sure like to get back now." "Well," he said, "if we get out alive, will you go back there with me?" I said, "Sure." I told him, "It'll take money." "Well," he said, "I'll get the money, just so long as you go along with me." So I said, "OK."

Sure enough, after the war he came back to Beaver. But that happened to be the year me and Sam Pingalo were on a wild goose chase over in the Koyukuk on another lost mine proposition.

When we finally got back to Beaver, why we heard that this fellow was there, the guy I met in the service the first night in Anchorage. He had grub, boat, and everything ready to go with me up the Hodzana. Of course, he started up the Hodzana, but, you know, greenhorn, cheechakar, he didn't get very far. He came back and left the boat there for me. So I never even did get a chance to see him. We were gone all summer, Sam and I.

But I did check up on his story and this is what I learned. Old Adam was the man from the Hodzana Country up there. He was born and raised up there and lived up there, oh, a good many years, almost a hundred years I guess. Now here's a story that is told about Old Adam, one of the stories that they tell which I checked with people here and there that I know well, and of course we don't know for sure, but this is what is handed down to us. And here I pass it on.[33]

91

It seems, now down at the mouth of the Hodzana, there used to be a darn good place for fishing. That's where Old Adam was fishing. And those days, those early days, my golly, the country was full of stampeders, you know. People came in boats that they made themselves. They came looking for a place to go prospecting. And one time there was a young man, a real young man who landed at Old Adam's fish camp there. And the old man took a liking to him right away. He tied up there and they fed him and everything. he had some dogs with him. Them days they had dogs too, you know. He had three dogs. So the old man told him to take his dogs off of there and tie them up. Those dogs got to rest.

So he stayed there two or three days, you know, and they got to talking, and this young man he made quite a hit with the old man. The old man liked him. He did work around the camp and he made bannocks and everything like that by the fire. That was what everybody used to eat in those days, bannocks. And you make it just right, why it still is good eating.

Well, anyway, they got to talking and Old Adam asked him, "What you looking for?" He says, "I'm looking for gold." And he took out his pocket poke. Everybody had a pocket poke them days, small pocket poke. He took out a little gold, a few pieces of gold that he had. "This is what I'm looking for." So Old Adam said, "Well, I'll take you up there, lots up there."

Anyway, the outcome was that they went up, upriver. He left his family there, his wife and his kids. The kids were big enough so they could look after camp. So the old man and this young man, they took off—lining and poling, no outboard motors those days. And they got up there and they came out in the fall, towards fall. They were gone, oh, I don't know, they were gone pretty near a month I guess. And they came back down and the young man, he stopped a steamboat. Them days you can stop a steamboat anyplace and you can buy an outfit from the purser if you've got the gold. Well, this young man would buy a good outfit for Old Adam, and old man would have all the grub he needs for the winter, ammunition and stuff like that. And the young man would cache his gold with the purser.

I don't know how much gold there was but it must have been quite a bit because this went on for four different seasons. And Old Man Adam, when he went to the trading post, after he got acquainted with this young man, he bought everything with gold, gold coins, twenty dollar gold pieces and ten dollar gold pieces. And then he had those great big, what they used to call "horse blankets." You know those bills? Yeah, that's what the young man gave him.

Anyway, that went on for about four different times and after that he never, he never did show up. So something must have happened to this young man. But Old Adam, up to the day he died he had gold. And the story is that there is still about four or five of those big baking powder cans full of gold, stashed away up there someplace, yeah. That's the story there.

Oh, I ask my brother-in-law, Solomon Adams, you know, stories come out about different people. There are a lot of stories about Old Adam. And I told my brother-in-law, I said, "Your dad, he's supposed to know where there's a lot of gold and he's got a lot of gold."

"Oh," he says, "that old so and so, yeah, he's got money. You should see him when he's around the trading post to buy grub. He pay for everything in gold, gold coin. And you try to ask him where he got that gold, he won't tell you a doggone thing. He won't tell nobody anything. When I found out the value of gold, when I was old enough to find out the value of gold, I try to ask him. He wouldn't tell me a doggone thing. He wouldn't tell. I tell him, 'How come?' Well he say he promise his Whiteman friend that he never tell anybody."

And those old-time Indians, you know, they'd die before they'd break their word. They're a different class of people from the Indians you see nowadays. So he would never tell nobody just where that gold is. And I don't know where it is, and I trapped and prospected up in there all these years. So far as I'm concerned, it's still up there, but I don't know where it is.

As I said, after I got out of the service, Sam Pingalo and I headed out to look for a lost mine. Sam was quite a prospector; he did a lot of prospecting. Besides that he was a natural-born mechanic. Everybody in that area over in that neck of the woods, anything wrong with any kind of machinery, they used to bring it to Sam Pingalo and he'd get it running. It seems that way back in 1914,-15,-16 around there, Sam was over

"That's Old Adam and his country is the Hodzana. He was born and raised there. He was a very independent man and stood up for his rights."

Well, we started out from the store there and then we just headed right straight over into the wilderness. Over creeks and hills and I don't know what all we went over with these great big packs. We lived off our packs and what small game we can kill. We didn't carry rifles, we carried handguns. Sam Pingalo, he had an old .45 Smith and Wesson model of 1917 and I had a .45 automatic Colt, and then I had a .22 Colt Woodsman. We depend on those guns to eat and we killed everything from ground squirrels to mountain sheep with them. So we lived good. We lived good in the woods. We covered a lot of territory in that time but we panned here and there and we looked everywhere, but I guess we just didn't look in the right place. We never did find that lost mine.

As I said, we were living off the country and this particular time we were getting short and we needed some fresh meat. We were working our way up the head of a creek. Sam had spotted a sheep way up at the head of the creek. We were down below and were going to start working our way up. So by the time we got near the head, why we dropped our packs there and worked our way up gradually. By golly, pretty near time for sheep to lay down. So we looked and sure enough, there was a great big ram laying down, way up there. So we started to sneak up, crawling on our bellies. Well, we crawled as far as we can under what cover we could find until we finally come out there where there's just nothing but rocks, and that darn sheep is right there in plain sight over there. We can't get any closer. We were laying down alongside each other. He says, "It's quite a good distance yet. Even with a 30-30, lucky you hit him that distance." "Well," I said to him, "we can't get any closer. I'm going to try to shoot from here."

I had that Colt Automatic National Match they call it. That's a hand finished action, supposed to be very acccurate .45 automatic. I took a full sight, we were laying flat on our stomachs. I took a full sight and I held over that. I held a full bead over and I squeezed the trigger. Then I see the dust raise just this side of him. Sheep always, when they're startled, there's a second when they freeze. Well, I took advantage of that. For my second shot I held a little higher. And in that second, you know, I took the same sight picture, raised it a little higher and I squeezed the trigger. And I noticed the head dropped like that. By golly, I hit it right in the spine, right here. One shot killed him deader than a door nail.

That was one of those lucky shots. You don't see one like that very often. It was a lucky shot, yeah.

So we had enough meat. We skinned out that sheep and we packed the meat down to where there's some dry wood and we dried out the meat and filled up on meat. Oh boy, we had a good time there, rested there a day taking care of that meat, you know. After it partially dried it was much lighter and easier to carry, yeah. So that was one lucky shot that we made.

Well, no more chasing around in the hills for gold. I got married, you know, and I have to work for a living.

*"That's the time Celia Hunter was over there too. She was the
moving spirit behind that Rural Development."*

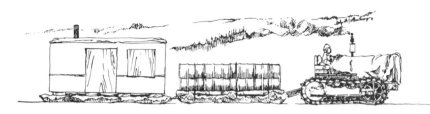

THE RURAL DEVELOPMENT PROJECT

It seems most of the people in Beaver wanted cabins. People been hollering for cabins for years and they finally got help, but they had to do most of the work themselves. They wrote down to Juneau and Mr. Gagnon, Mr. Paul Gagnon came around to see what the conditions were and then that's where I met Mr. Gagnon.[35] He wanted somebody to take charge, you know. And I told him what experience I had with Mr. Nicholson building and how I learned to operate a small sawmill. Well, he told me, "Do you want to take charge here?" I says, "Well sure, I'll tackle the job." So, that's how we started there, yeah.

Then they sent two old cats there, D-7 cats that the Army been using building the highway up here to Alaska.[36] They got them to Beaver. Of course, they needed to be worked over, you know. They were pretty well worn out but they were still able to work. And we used them all the time on this building and sawmill and logging and all that.

There was one man there named Clinton Wiehl. Well, ever since he was a kid down at Rampart, you know, that's all he did was ride those cats and learn about them. Why, they did a lot of mining in those days in Rampart with those cats, that's where he learned. By golly, he knew his job. Me, I didn't know beans about cats, but he was the one. And Mr. Gagnon told him, "You work with Moses here." So that's the deal he made. Clinton looked after the cats. We worked for the State for a couple of seasons that time.

After about a year and a half of work over there at Beaver on the building project, the people in Arctic Village wanted the same kind of deal up there. So our boss from Juneau, Mr. Paul Gagnon, wanted to know if we could take the equipment up to Arctic Village, me and Clint. Those old cats, they needed to be worked over. Why, Clinton, he knew just what to do, but then there's so much work to be done, parts got to be replaced. They asked Clint, "Could you put them in?" And he said, "Sure, if you give me the parts."

So he did. I was his helper. I remember all the parts that Clint ordered. That list was a mile long, and when we finally started on those cats, he had that darn thing scattered all over. I was wondering how in the world he could ever put it back together again. But I helped him, and we worked eight, ten, sometimes twelve hours a day. We got paid for eight, but we worked ten, sometimes worked twelve hours a day. And we worked sometimes six days a week. We always took Sundays off. Because this was a project that was helping our people and it helped us there in the village so this extra work we did, we didn't mind that at all.

By gosh, he had those darn old cats, all the parts scattered all over there, and new parts come in there, and he put them in and by golly, they worked. Well anyway, after a month or so, a little over a month working on these cats, finally we got them all together. And then we had to build our equipment for this trip. We had to build sleds made out of big logs, wannigans.[37] All that we built. Some of the old cable we had there, we used that, everything just homemade. The State didn't have that much money to buy the kind of equipment which was needed. But we did good. I never seen anything like it. Always when there's machines, you expect some kind of mechanical trouble. We didn't have one bit of mechanical trouble all the way from Beaver to Arctic Village, not one bit.

Anyway, we finally got the cats in running order and after we got through with the cats, they sent a man over from NC. I forgot his name. Oh, he was a darn good guy. He was one of the mechanics there at the NC cat department. He came over and he checked our work on the cats, and he said, "Boys, I couldn't have done it better myself. I don't see nothing wrong with it. Everything seems to be in first-class shape and you boys did a good job in this repair." I forgot his name, oh, he was well liked, old Alaskan, you know. And I told him, I says, "I'm no cat skinner. I can handle that little sawmill out there. I can handle a pick and shovel, but I'm no cat man." He laughed and he says, "Moses, I think by the time you get up to Arctic Village you'll be able to drive one of these cats."

And then we told him about the trip and I asked him, "How long do

*"That's our 'cat train.' By golly that's me on that 'cat' there.
That's Ambrose Williams. He knows that country up there."*

"Oh yes, here's Clint and I. Clint, he's the 'cat' man. He's the one that taught me."

you think it will take us?" He hit it right square on the head. I forgot, twenty-three or twenty-seven days, I think twenty-three days. "Twenty-three days, it will take you boys twenty-three days, yeah, if everything goes well, you know." Well, anyway, he wished us luck and everything and then he took off. We were all ready to take off then. We pulled a load, hauled our equipment, sawmill, tools and what fuel we had.

Oh, before we started, there's two boys that flew down from Arctic Village to help us, Kias Peter and Ambrose Williams. These boys knew that country up there. They were born and raised in that country and they trapped that country all their lives. And they knew that country well. And without them we would have probably never made it because they knew all the best places to go, even some of those places that were real rugged. Why if that was the best place to go, we went there. And they were a big help to us.

And then we didn't even have something to heat up the engines in the morning. Lucky we had five of those great big insulated army tents. They're the warmest darn thing you can think of. You know in the evenings when we quit, we throw this big tent right over the cat; it fits over with a lot of room to spare, all the way down to the ground. It's just like airtight. And this insulated tent, it kept that doggone engine warm all night. And even that, if it was cold we got up about four o'clock in the morning and we built a little campfire underneath it. Why in about fifteen or twenty minutes, the doggone engine is warm. And by golly, one crank on the starting engine and the engine takes right off, and then we switch on the diesels. Why they just take right off too. The State was short on money them days, you know, we didn't have much of an outfit. We didn't have, well, we had nothing to warm up the engines with, and I guess those guys down there, I guess they thought we would never even get to Venetie, you know.[38] Anyway, we made it to Venetie and here was a Herman Nelson heater for us, yeah, a brand new one. Oh man, no trouble heating up the cats after that.

You know, that's the one thing that I really wonder about. Since we left, we didn't have one bit of mechanical trouble, all the way up to Arctic Village. And boy we went through some rugged country, some places right straight up the mountain sides and right straight down through timber in the Sheep Mountains.

We could follow the road out thirty miles, out that old horse trail from Beaver there, but from there we turned off, and then we're on our own. You know, that's rugged country up that way. There's no roads we could follow. No kind of a trail or a darn thing, rivers, mountains, everything like that to cross.

I remember one time it took us all morning and round about one or two o'clock, we reached a summit and it's kind of a clearing there. And a storm came up and we just can't see each other. We already made plans in case of emergency, for everything we planned ahead. In case of something like that we were to form a circle, and I was on this side and he was on that side. So he turned and we stopped right there. And then he told me, this one time, we had to keep the engines running.

You know, on the regular cat train—when bum weather—they got a lot of fuel, they can idle their engines all night. And Clint, he's the boss, you know. He's the cat man. He said, "Moses we'll keep our engines running." By golly, by that time the wind almost knock us off our cats. We had canvas fastened down solid so the wind didn't tear them up, but how in the world that wannigan stayed on that sled, I don't know. It was nailed down see. It was spiked down solid. Well, we can't see each other, we had to holler. We can't walk. When we left our cats after we get in this circle, you can't stand up, the wind will knock you flat on your back, yup. We crawled back to the wannigan.

And then after we got in the game country, lots of caribou. We lived high. We were kind of working on short rations. As I said, the State didn't have much money, but when we got into caribou country we had all we wanted to eat then.

Well, anyway, we finally got up to Arctic Village. At that time, they had some sort of a radio station so that they could contact our people in any town in Alaska.

So the first thing I did after we got to Arctic Village was to send a message to my boss, Paul Gagnon. He was supposed to have gone with us on this trip but before the trip started, they called a special session and all the department heads had to be there so he couldn't go. And oh, he wanted in the worst way to go along. According to what I found out afterwards, why everyone of those guys down there where they're making those laws, it seems like every darn one of them was one time or another a cat skinner. And they told him that we would never in God's world make it up to Arctic Village. They said those two old cats like that, and through that rugged country, we would never make it.

Well it was rugged country all right, but we were lucky, we made it. And I sent this message to him by radio there. It so happened, he told me afterwards that they were in this session, and just as soon as he got the message, why he tried to get their attention so he could read it. He finally got their attention and he read the message to them and he said you could hear a pin drop. Those guys that said we would never make it, why, they didn't know what to say.

Well, anyway, all kinds of orders came. The BIA wanted lakes cleared of snow so they could land equipment there, and there was a lot of clearing to do.[39] The people already had a lot of logs cut and all those logs have to be hauled in and I got to rig up the sawmill. But the first thing that we did was to clear out these airfields. This one cat was rigged up so it had a big blade, so it could do a good job of clearing in no time at all. This other cat was rigged up with a power takeoff for operating the sawmill, yeah. Well, we got started. We worked eight or ten, ten hours a day at the first, getting started, clearing off those fields. And then all kinds of stuff came in for the BIA, building materials and all kinds of stuff. We kept hauling, oh my gosh, day and night until they finally got all the stuff up there. And then they were able to put up that school there and a lot of other stuff the village needed. The arrival of those cats up there made possible the building of that school.

Anyway, logs had to be hauled in. We took two cats out and we hauled in a bunch of logs. And then I rigged up the sawmill and Clint, he kept hauling logs with the other cat, and I picked out my crew and tried to teach them the safe way to work around a sawmill. Well, I had four or five men in the crew there, you know. Finally we got the mill set up and started sawing. The first log I had on there, well, I put it through the mill and they all started laughing. They laughed their heads off! So I stopped the saw and I said, "What's the matter?" "Why," they said, "before, if we wanted to get a piece of lumber, it took us all day to saw one or two. Now, in less than a few seconds, you saw a piece of board." They thought that was great.

Well, anyway, we started sawing there and we turned out a first class crew there; they caught on fast. Inside of a week's time we had a lot of logs and lumber cut, stuff like that. And all the time Clint hauling in with the other cat. So, we had enough stuff cut there and logs; we squared enough logs so that people could really start on their jobs and we got everything going. Then they ran out of money. There was absolutely no more money for that project. So the project was called off for a while. But by that time the BIA had their building up there, and the people had their houses started, and they had a big pile of lumber cut. So they were able to go ahead and they built some pretty neat cabins up there, yeah.

When I came back I went to work for the BIA. I had a year-round job. I was maintenance man over there at Beaver. And I worked for years until I was retired.[40] I was lucky though, I had a month off every summer with full pay. And I spent that time prospecting up the Hodzana.

*"Those people are really dedicated, fine people to work with.
They're all interested in the kids."*

FAIRBANKS AND THE
FAIRBANKS NATIVE ASSOCIATION

I didn't want to quit work but the law made me retire. And my retirement—it costs me so much to live out in the bush country you know, everything, everything has to be brought in by airplane and the freight is sky high. So my wife, she wanted to come over here in the worst way, and well, we thought we'd come over here. I had been here quite a number of times before, way back in the early days too. We decided to move to Fairbanks because I was retired from work and we thought it would be cheaper to live. So that's how come we moved over here, over here to Fairbanks.

Oh, my gosh, it's changed so much from the early days. I just can't hardly believe my eyes sometimes when I see all the change that has taken place here. I remember driving into Fairbanks with my dog team when I was driving dogs for our ministers, dog team days. And now when I look around at all the—what they call improvements and everything like that—all the building that's going on, I just can't hardly believe my eyes sometimes.

Here in town I've been working with the Fairbanks Native Association[41] and I enjoy working with the youngsters, you know, telling them about the early days and how the people used to live and all that stuff. Well, they like to hear stories about travelling with dogs out on the trails, about hunting and trapping, and stuff like that. They enjoy that and I enjoy working with FNA, yes.

Well, I've been asked questions about the early days and about my life and I'm glad to recall things like that because I know that's the only way it could be recorded. And I think it's pretty good that people have interest and if I can in anyway help along that line, I'm glad to do all I can to help.

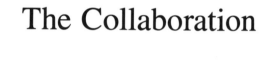
The Collaboration

A LIFETIME OF HISTORY

Moses Cruikshank was born at Fishhook Town, a place now commonly called Chalkyitsik. This is a small Native village on the Black River, a tributary of the Porcupine. The exact date of his birth is unknown, some say 1902, others have it down as 1906. He grew up learning the Athabaskan traditions of his family, and he never forgot the importance of their lessons. Grandpa Henry's presence is felt throughout the narrative—in lessons of how to hunt and take care of game, proper care of guns, and in personal qualities such as firmness in the face of adversity and willingness to share with others. The experiences of this old man bridged the Native and White world and their recounting by Moses reminds us how long Athabaskans on the Yukon and the Porcupine rivers have lived with Whitemen and their ways.

Where Grandpa Henry lived, there had been direct contact with Western traders since the 1840's. Russian fur traders reached Nulato on the lower Yukon in 1839 and the Hudson's Bay Company established Fort Yukon in 1847 at the confluence of the Porcupine and Yukon rivers. But even before the 1840's, Athabaskans on the Yukon acquired western goods in exchange for their furs. They travelled many miles outside their home territory and they also traded with "middlemen," Native traders who moved back and forth between the western traders and the Native groups, exchanging fur for items like metal knives, beads, and cloth. [42]

Grandpa Henry and his parents were familiar with Whitemen and their ways. But the stampeders at the turn of the century were quite different from the traders and prospectors that came before, men who knew how to live off the country.

First Stampeders

When the stampeders arrived there were a few years when the country was pretty wild. Hundreds of men made their way from camp to camp—some quite unprepared to live off the country. Moses tells us how Grandpa Henry generously gave fish to those who stopped at the camp but kept a cautious eye for the ones that might make trouble.

In those days prospectors followed three routes to the Upper Yukon: the old Hudson's Bay Company river and portage trails from the Mackenzie drainage to the Peel and down the Porcupine, by ocean steamer to St. Michael and riverboat up the Yukon; or from Skagway over the Chilkoot trail to the head of the Yukon

113

and thence downstream. The few trading posts were supplied by river steamer from St. Michael. For some of the Indians living along the river, the Gold Rush meant pressure on game resources, shortages of trade goods and higher prices at the trading posts. [43] Always looking for the big find, most stampeders didn't stay long in one place. That's simply the nature of prospecting. At the more productive mining camps on the Yukon, places like Circle and Rampart, miners settled in and worked for wages. And these areas are still being worked today.

Soon after the turn of the century, when the good prospects on the Yukon were staked, prospectors made their way to the tributary streams—the Koyukuk and the Tanana, where paying quantities of gold were reported. Fairbanks, located a short way up the Chena, a tributary of the Tanana, eventually became a supply center for prospectors and mining interests in the Tanana Valley. [44]

Beaver developed and prospered at the river terminus of a road north to the Upper Koyukuk and Chandalar gold fields. Today the old wagon trail north to the Chandalar is still visible in places and the few rusting wagon wheels and accounts of old-timers like Moses remind us of the early history of that town and the people who called it home. [45]

Development of the Trapping Economy

Most of the prospectors who came in search of gold left empty handed. A few found good ground and became wealthy, others turned to wage work, and still others made a living by trapping along with Indians for whom hunting, fishing, and trapping was an established way of life. Grandpa Henry's son, Paul Henry, took over his father's rich trapping country up the Porcupine, and along with the many others—Native and White—helped establish the Upper Yukon as a major fur trapping center. As Moses grew up, he watched the transition to a full time fur trapping economy—a way of life he describes in the account of wintering with Paul Henry and trapping with his brother-in-law, Solomon Adams. Interior trappers followed a yearly pattern of fishing and wood cutting in the summer, fall hunting and supply of the line cabins, and then a winter of trapping. The long winter was broken up by the Christmas trip to town; that was the time to get supplies, bring in fur, visit, and celebrate the holidays. The holidays provided relief from the isolation of the trapline and families looked forward to visiting when they came to town. In those days, families didn't spend much time in town.

When Moses returned from the Army he settled back into a trapper's life. His brother-in-law's children were by then of school age and his sister, Charlotte, and the children were in Beaver so the children could attend school. The establishment of village schools meant that the families were split up during the winter— the women and children in the village during the school year and the men out on the trapline.

The Development of Mission Schools

Many years before, when Moses was taken in by the mission at Fort Yukon, schools were an exception and they weren't found in small villages. Parents and children headed out together on the trapline and there was little thought of schooling. The mission schools were originally established as part of the church's goal to provide health care and education along with spiritual instruction. Children like Moses in need of medical care, or orphans and youngsters whose parents were having trouble supporting them, were taken in by the mission schools. Fort Yukon became a mission center. Dr. Burke, the medical missionary who helped Moses, came to Fort Yukon in 1908 and devoted his life to the medical and spiritual care of people in that part of the Interior. [46] When he wasn't on the trail, Archdeacon Stuck also spent time at Fort Yukon, writing and ministering to the people.

Parents and members of the community helped the missions by making contributions of fish and meat and when possible, donating money. But as Moses relates, the children worked hard cutting wood, fishing, and hauling meat. These were the first schools in Alaska and men like Archdeacon Stuck were careful to note that the church mission schools must never separate the children from the skills of living on the land. He put it this way:

"Moreover, it is folly to fail to recognize that the apprenticeship of an Indian boy to the arts by which he must make a living, the arts of hunting and trapping, is more important than schooling, however important the latter may be, and that any talk—and there has been loud talk—of a compulsory education law which shall compel such boys to be in school at times when they should be off in the wilds with their parents, is worse than folly, and would, if carried out, be a fatal blunder. If such boys grow up incompetent to make a living out of the surrounding wilderness, whence shall their living come?" [47]

Unfortunately, in later years when the public school systems were developed, this point was overlooked. The separation of children from life out on the land has continued to the present. [48]

Mission Travel

In the Interior, the strong tradition of mission outreach was started by Church of England clergy, men such as Archdeacon McDonald and the Reverend Sim. They thought nothing of heading out on foot for lengthy trips to camps and villages where their parishioners were living. Archdeacon Stuck, the most famous Episcopal clergyman, continued this tradition. He travelled extensively by dog team in winter and on the *Pelican*, the church boat in summer. His books provide a running account of the places he went and the conditions they found. Moses' recounting of this period is presented from two perspectives, that of a young man growing up in the church and learning how to handle dogs and from the standpoint of an older man looking back at the changes he has experienced. From the standpoint of the second perspective, Moses realizes what people who didn't experience that travel need to know to understand life then. This is what makes his descriptions so valuable. He bridges the reality of travel before airplanes to life today. In the course of describing his personal experiences we come to realize the means of travel, the trails and some of the people who lived

*"That's Archdeacon Stuck, yes. He was quite a walker too. He
start out early in the morning ahead on snowshoes. That way the
dogs will have a good trail, till they catch up with him anyway."*

along the way. Only through such personal description can we gain a sense for the conditions of travel and the networks that linked people together.

New Routes to the Interior

In many respects the church's development of mission stations in the Interior followed the mineral and economic development of the territory—first the Yukon Valley missions, then the tributary streams, the Koyukuk and the Tanana valleys. When Moses was transferred to the mission at Nenana, this village was becoming a hub of activity for Interior Alaska.

The story of how Nenana developed goes back to the stampeders at the turn of the century. The Army was looking for an "American" overland route to the Yukon, to alleviate problems of supply. As early as 1897 some army men were talking about building a railroad through the Interior to Tanana on the Yukon River. William Yanert, the old-timer from Purgatory, led one of the first military explorations and described the route eventually chosen for the Alaska Railroad. The railroad never reached the Yukon but it has played a major role in the development of the Interior.

Nenana is where the railroad line reached the Tanana River. Trains brought in supplies from ice-free tide water and in summer steamboats headed out from Nenana to supply the villages of the Yukon.

The significance of the railroad in providing access to the Interior is dramatically illustrated by Moses' personal experiences. As a young boy he travelled with the ministers on the church boat down to the mouth of the Yukon so they could catch the ocean steamer for outside. That trip took many days and once the missionaries got on the steamer they had to travel around the west coast of Alaska before heading south to Seattle. Years later, when he went outside to school, Moses travelled on the new railroad—a quick trip to Anchorage where he got on a steamship for Seattle. The new route saved many miles and much time.

Fairbanks: from Camp to Town

As a young man Moses came to Fairbanks and worked in the mines at Chatanika and Livengood. Unlike his own prospecting activities, these were proven commerical ventures supported by mining companies with large investors' interests backing them up. Mineral development in Alaska is marked by several distinct stages. Initial discovery, stampede and claim staking, and then either the area played out, supported a low but steady number of prospectors and small scale miners, or was profitable enough economically to attract big-money interests. With big-money support for the mines in the Tanana Valley, the development of Fairbanks looked promising. But as Bill Stroecker, a pioneer banker points out, for many years people continued to think of Fairbanks as a camp. No one was sure it would ever become a town with any permanence. But then, the World War II buildup swelled the payrolls and the University began to grow and in time the economy became diversified enough to provide a stable economic base. [49]

117

Military Service

World War II brought big changes to Fairbanks. Establishment of military bases and construction of the Alaska Highway meant more people and greater access to the State. The war effort also brought changes to villages. Moses, like many other rural Alaskans who served during World War II, takes pride in his contribution to the military defense of the nation. Many Natives shared freely their survival skills. The introduction of Native footgear, mitts, and gun cases are an example of this. As the war came closer to the Alaskan mainland, the personal survival skills of rural Alaskans were considered very important. There was considerable pride in the Alaskan troops. [50]

Military service brought hundreds of men together from all over Alaska. Perhaps that was the first time so many rural Alaskans had gathered together at one time. Friendships formed during this period continue to the present.

Military service provided opportunities to learn new skills and to travel to many other parts of the world. The experiences were also valuable in preparing rural Alaskans to participate in program opportunities during the postwar period. Men learned how large military organizations work and they found out how to get things done in the system, whether it be contacting a legislator to get fair treatment, or applying for funds to run a program in a local community. Military experience widened the horizons of villagers and some of today's leaders were young soldiers during the war. When it ended they saw ways of benefiting their home communities through participation in regional, territorial and national programs, and they applied their experiences to that end.

Government Programs

The war changed a lot of things about Alaska. It brought new roads, better airfields, and greater national attention to the territory. Alaska was visible, important, and accessible to Americans. Growing attention on Alaska was reflected in government programs. The Alaska Rural Development Program is an example at the legislative level of a growing interest in bringing services to rural Alaskans. The project was designed to provide the means for people to build new houses. Of central concern to the project sponsors was that new housing be dry, warm, and uncrowded. This would help combat tuberculosis, a major health problem for villagers, and an area where the medical profession was committed to finding cures. Marvelous advances were made in this area during the post war period. [51]

The housing project in Beaver was very successful. In fact, most of the houses built during that period are still used today, 26 years later. When it was completed in 1959, the project was considered a model for other villages.

On a map of Beaver produced for the report on the housing project, the streets are listed as Alaskan Way, 49th Street, and State Street, a tribute to the Alaska Statehood Movement which was underway at that time. The names didn't stick in Beaver but statehood paved the way for many new changes—not the least of which were the Alaska Native Claims Settlement Act, and decisions on the National Interest Lands. [52] In the last twenty-five years there has been growing

118

concern over the State's natural resources, and a growing concern of subsistence users over rights to hunting, fishing, and trapping. It has been a critical period for Native leaders who are called upon to make far-reaching decisions about the land and the resources upon which villagers depend.[53]

A Personal Recollection

The rural development work really was the last big story in Moses' account but it would be misleading to think that was the end of his active role in public affairs.

One of my earliest recollections of Moses is from 1973 when a group of village elders were gathered in the back of the small Episcopal Chruch in Beaver. They were there to make land selections for the village. Moses was standing up close to the map, squinting through his glasses to see the detail. His rough and worn fingers followed the river bank of the Yukon, downriver past the mouth of the Hodzana. Finally, he looked up and began to speak. His words were clear and direct, his voice strong and firm. "We should choose this area; it is good moose hunting country; we depend upon that meat for our livelihood."

As he spoke, the leaders listened knowing his experience on the land and trusting his judgement in dealing with government people. Questions about the land had always been settled between families but now the government and Native corporations were involved. There had been many meetings with agency officials that year and Moses commanded respect from these visitors.

Moses Cruikshank realized the importance of the land selections, and like the other men at the meeting, he drew upon his knowledge of the land, the habits of the animals, and the needs of villagers. But unlike the others gathered there, Moses' experiences included many years living and working with missionaries, prospectors and miners, military officers and government men. Comfortable in both the Native and non-Native world, Moses provided counsel to the younger leaders, encouraging them to speak up and to work for the community.

In the years since the land claims there have been many more meetings and I've heard Moses speak up on many issues. Firmly he stresses the need of villagers and old-time Alaskans to continue their way of life on the land without interference and regulations. "Old-time Alaskans" is his special way of pointing out people who have lived in Alaska long enough to prove themselves over the years; they're trustworthy, deserving of respect and consideration. For him the expression cuts across distinctions of Native and White, urban and rural, rich and poor. They're men like Grandpa Henry, Bob Bartlett, and the NC "cat" man.

Moses' willingness to serve as a public spokesman is a reflection of his senior position in the community and of a realization that his lifetime of experiences are important in addressing present concerns. His lifetime of diverse experiences prepares him to work well with Natives and Whites in rural Alaska and in the city; with those educated in schools and those educated in schools and those educated in the woods; and with the very young and the elderly. Moses bridges their experiences and he is respected by all of these people because they know he has experienced a bit of their life.

STORIES, TAPES, AND TEXTS

For many years I have wanted to record and write Moses Cruikshank's life history. The idea first came up in a conversation back in 1976 when my mother and I were visiting in Beaver. We had taken a short boat trip down to the point below Beaver and as we were walking along the beach, Moses' niece, Margaret Ann Fisher, mentioned to my mother that it would be good to document Uncle Moses' life. As I recall, Moses didn't object, but at that point he had other interests. Over the years he has voiced more and more interest in preserving history, and I have been privileged to work with him, recording his experiences, and developing this book. He has contributed many hours recording his life story, proofreading the text, and identifying and labeling photographs.

The stories in Moses' narrative have been told many times and to the seasoned listener there are few surprises, yet each telling is exciting. Like other good story tellers, Moses is reflective and doesn't take life for granted. His stories are full of personal experiences, carefully shaped to give the listener a blend of description, opinion, advice, and humor. And he tells them with authority, and a sense of the importance of each telling. He has the marvelous quality of being able to remember experiences from way back. This is the substance of the stories but it is important to recognize that he has distilled the episodes into a story form which is more than a rendering of details. The process occurs over many years spent thinking about experiences and distinguishing those parts he wants to share with other people—to teach a lesson, to tell what life was like under certain conditions and to provide perspective on the past and the present.

His close attention to detail and frequent use of qualifiers such as: "I remember," or "this is the story that has been handed down," or "I'm telling what I experienced" alert us to how he learned what he is about to say and the care he takes in passing on traditional knowledge.

Life Story or History

This book is a combination of life story and life history. Life stories emphasize the spoken word of the narrator and are presented in the first person. The storyteller tells his own story, in his own words, and in his own way. An interviewer may ask questions but the direction of the work comes from the narrator whose storytelling is considered intrinsically interesting and a contribution in and of itself, regardless of its truth. Life histories, on the other hand, are analytic and

121

interpretive. They are derived from the narrator's experiences but are evaluated through the lens of the writer whose training enables him to point out how the facts presented by the narrator enhance our understanding of areas such as history, culture, or personality. [54]

One can think of this book as a life history based on a life story. Moses tells his own story in his own way. I have "ordered" his stories chronologically, have provided footnotes to describe details which may be unknown to some readers, and I have described how his accounts contribute to an understanding of Alaskan history.

Life histories are historically important because they connect the "distant" past with the present. The connection is made through the life of an individual whose experiences span that time.

A good life history gives us a sense of how the person felt as he met people and experienced events which we recognize as historically important but rather distant from our own experiences. For instance, people like Archdeacon Stuck of the Episcopal Church is a man who is well-known for his books on Alaska but he becomes familiar to us in new ways as we learn how Moses knew him.

A good life history also provides the reader with an accurate feel for some of the personal influences which shaped the teller's life. This includes their hopes and dreams, and some of the people who were role models or provided help and encouragement along the way. The influence of parents, grandparents and other relatives extend the time depth of a life history, allowing us to see beyond the individual's life, to those who came before and the conditions of their lives.

Most life histories closely follow the life cycle. This includes birth, childhood, adolescence, adulthood, and old age. Each person's life is also influenced by cultural, historical, and situational factors which determine the particular content of a life history. In the case of life histories based exclusively on oral history, the narrator has the primary responsibility for determining content and the writer records, compiles, and edits the transcripts into the written narrative. There are, of course, many variations in how the narrator and writer collaborate, but in all cases, the emphasis is on preserving a sense of the teller speaking in his or her own words about what he or she thinks is important.

In Moses' story there's a great deal more we'd like to know, topics of a personal nature—his family life as a small boy, the pain of being separated from family, marriage, and child rearing. It isn't his way to speak publicly about these matters, about how he felt. Instead, he shares with us the values he tries to live by—hard work, conservation, honesty and perseverance. This is how we come to know him.

The Narrative

After hearing Moses' stories many times, I recognized that particular episodes could be introduced several ways depending upon his interest. A single story could serve as the basis for launching into several other episodes. A challenge in writing them down was to decide which stories should follow in this particular compilation. When Moses tells stories, he decides the order depending upon the point to be made, the audience present, and his inclination. What I have tried to do is string the stories together in sets with subheadings to guide the reader. Each set contains several accounts, connected when possible in ways he has connected them on past occasions.

Moses' stories are really comparable to the rare diary or letters found in archival collections; they provide a glimpse of his life. And yet, the stories differ from archival collections because they are told over and over again; they have a life of their own and the telling is influenced by factors such as who is present, the conversations that have come before, and the particular point that Moses wants to make. In telling a hunting story he may emphasize to strangers the fact that not one bit of meat was wasted, but to relatives and friends he may concentrate on telling who was on the hunt and where they went. In putting these stories down in a written form they become set in a particular way. Unfortunately, there's no chance for you, the reader, to be present when Moses begins a story, to see his eyes light up, to watch him sit forward in his seat and then to hear him begin by saying, "you know," and then to launch full bore into a well chosen account to illustrate his point. [55]

The recordings that serve as the basis for this narrative were made in the Oral History Office of the Elmer Rasmuson Library and in my home. The setting is quite removed from the usual places where Moses tells stories. Unlike the usual storytelling context, he told me these stories at my prompting. I encouraged him to tell particular stories that I had heard before. One taping session he brought a list of old-timers and told a little bit about each one and where they lived. These comments were inserted to enrich the discussion of places where he went with the missionaries.

Complete transcripts were made of the recordings and played back, and I read the transcripts as I listened to the tapes. Punctuation and emphasis changes were made to correspond as closely as possible to Moses' spoken word. False starts and stutters were eliminated. Some repetitions were removed but his grammatical style was maintained as much as possible. The transcripts and tapes are now available for public use in the Alaska and Polar Regions Department Archives at the Elmer Rasmuson Library, University of Alaska, Fairbanks.

After I completed the transcripts, I recognized that I could piece the stories together into a narrative of Moses' life. I found it necessary to cross-check a few details, to seek greater elaborations, and in some cases to look for bridges which would link several accounts covering a particular period of his life.

The narrative was edited extensively for readability. When it was necessary for me to add words or phrases to connect episodes, I tried to choose words that Moses would use. In most cases, the editing process involved cutting out repetitions that seemed to slow the written story down. Repetitions in speech are a common way of emphasizing a point, but in the written form, the reader finds repetitions tedious and distracting. Deciding how much repetition to include was difficult but it forced me to consider readers and their special needs.

One of the more radical things I did in the narrative was to combine elements from similar episodes, enriching the narrative description with as much detail as I could find in the recordings. For instance, the story of Old Adam was told several times and I combined elements from each telling in the written narrative. It's possible that Moses might sit down and tell the entire narrative at one sitting in the order produced here, including all the descriptive parts. It would be a long evening, and it would depend upon many other factors, not the least of which is the audience, a consideration of who is present and their responses.

Audience

As I put these stories together, my thoughts turned to the people who would read this book. My first consideration was Moses; his agreement and identification with the arrangement was critical because I wanted it to remain his story. But there are other audiences too: his contemporaries in the village and in Fairbanks, the young relative who today is listening to him tell about shooting the big bear with Chief Christian, members of the Episcopal Church who may have heard a small bit about the church's activities in Alaska and longed to hear more, students of Alaskan history and anthropology who want to hear first hand about life in the Interior, folklorists interested in the art of storytelling and the large number of people who I suspect would enjoy sitting down with Moses and listening for an hour or so as he told some of these stories. The book has been organized with these people in mind. [56]

FOOTNOTES

1. Stampeders are gold seekers who came north in search of riches and adventure. There was very little in the way of law and order in the Interior of Alaska, even after the United States Army arrived and set up forts in 1899 at Tanana (Fort Gibbon) and Eagle (Fort Egbert).

2. Blunt tipped arrows made out of bone or spent cartridges were used to stun the waterfowl.

3. Stickmen or brushmen look like people and in some ways act like men but they are considered wild. Sometimes they scare people out in the woods. There are many Athabaskan stories about stickmen and how they bother women and children but no one has ever captured or killed one of these beings.

4. The Hudson's Bay Company was the leading English fur trading company. Chartered in 1670, this company established posts all across Canada, finally entering Alaska and establishing Fort Yukon in 1847. This was the farthest west of their posts and was located clearly within Russian held territory, that is until the Treaty of Cession in 1867 and then was in trespass on land where American jurisdiction held. When the Company's right to the post was challenged in 1869 by an American Army officer, the Company factor moved the trading post up the Porcupine River to a spot closer to the Canadian line but still within Alaska. It was not until years after that the Hudson's Bay Company actually moved out of Alaska.

5. The Russian-American Company established a trading post at Nulato in 1838.

6. Gold was discovered in the Circle area in 1893 and the town of Circle soon grew up around Jack McQuesten's trading post. Further information about the Circle area can be acquired from the Circle-Central Museum and from Pat Oakes who lives in Central and is working on local history in that area.

7. NC stands for Northern Commercial Company, a large chain of trading stores which began operations in Alaska in 1867. See *Flag Over the North* by L.D. Kitchener, 1954, Seattle, Superior Publishing Co.

8. Archdeacon Stuck describes his trip up the Mountain in *The Ascent of Denali*, 1914, New York, Charles Scribner's Sons.

9. The Kantishna and Toklat rivers flow from the foothills of the Alaska Range into the Tanana River. These are considered some of the finest game hunting areas in the Interior. Game was hunted here by Natives as well as by suppliers of meat to butcher shops in Fairbanks, during the early part of this century.

10. Father Julius Jetté was a Catholic priest stationed at Nulato during all but one of the years from 1898 to 1906. He was then reassigned to Tanana. He is well-remembered for his years of service on the river and for documenting the Koyukon language and culture. He was respected for his personal fluency and his willingness to preach in Koyukon. For more information see Louis Renner's article, "Julius Jetté: Distinguished Scholar in Alaska...a Jesuit priest and accomplished linguist on the Yukon." in *Alaska Journal*, Vol. 5, no. 4, p. 239-247.

11. Nenana was a good place to find work when the railroad was being built. When it was completed, Nenana was the river terminus for the trains and steamboats. From Nenana, steamboats headed out for the Yukon with freight brought up on the railroad. Wage work was available on the docks, the steamboats, and the railroad.

12. Wheel dogs are harnessed closest to the sled. They're the heavy pullers.

13. Before airplanes became readily available in Alaska (circa 1939), the mail was carried by dog teams. A system of roadhouses along the winter trail provided shelter for mail carriers and other travellers. The mail carriers were expected to make a certain number of trips so they had to break trail, no matter how much snow. (For more information on airplanes in Alaskan history see, *The Flying North* by Jean Potter, 1947, New York, The Macmillan Company.)

14. William Yanert was a member of the 1898 Tanana River Exploring Expedition and personally led one of the most important traverses up the Susitna River from Cook Inlet toward Broad Pass near present day Cantwell. The route he mapped out on this expedition was later followed by the Alaska Railroad and the George Parks Highway. (See *Compilation of Narratives of Explorations in Alaska*, 1900, Washington, Government Printing Office, p. 677-679.)

15. Frank Yasuda and his wife Nevalo came to Beaver in 1910 with several Eskimo families. Frank set up a trading post where he thought the government would build a road north to the mining areas around Wiseman, Caro, and Chandalar. A wagon trail was actually built from Beaver north to the mining areas. Parts of the old road are still visible, although the old cabins along the trail have deteriorated with time. For more information on the history of Beaver see William Schneider's *Beaver, Alaska: The Story of a Multi-Ethnic Community*, 1976, Ph.D. dissertation, Bryn Mawr College.

16. Bannock is a variation of fried bread made with flour, water, grease or butter and baking powder or baking soda. Ingredients like eggs and raisins or other dried fruit are sometimes added. Bannocks can be made in a frying pan over an open campfire.

17. The gee pole extends out from the front of the sled and is used to keep a heavily loaded sled on the trail.

18. Babiche is thin strips of moose hide which is soaked in water to make it pliable and then it is used to lash sled parts together, and for snowshoe webbing. When the babiche dries it shrinks and tightens the lashing thereby creating a secure yet flexible fastening.

19. Tanana Crossing is now called Tanacross.

20. The Pioneer Hotel and the Model Cafe were well known and frequented by folks coming in to Fairbanks off the trail.

21. Mt. Hermon is a college preparatory school for boys and several other boys raised in the Episcopal missions went there: Arthur Wright, Walter Harper and John Fredson.

22. The spike boy laid out the spikes along the track and then the men would come along and drive them in. The water boy carried water for the crews to drink.

23. Bob Bartlett was elected territorial delegate to Congress in 1945 and represented Alaskans in Washington for 23 years, first as a delegate and then as a senator. (See Claus Naske's *Bob Bartlett of Alaska-A Life in Politics*, 1979, Fairbanks, University of Alaska Press, p. 65, 175, 238.)

24. The Alaska Railroad was completed in 1923.

25. Before outboard motors, boats were pulled upstream by hand or by dogs in harness. Boats were also propelled upstream by the use of long poles pushing off the stream bed. These methods were called lining and poling.

26. Moses uses the word "outfit" to refer to equipment and supplies as well as a group of people working together.

27. John Minook found gold in the Rampart area in 1893. (See Alfred Hulse Brooks' *Blazing Alaska's Trails*, 1953, Fairbanks, University of Alaska Press, p. 332.)

    Donald Orth reports Minook Creek, "Named in the early 1890's by prospectors for John Minook, 'Russian halfbreed,' who is reported to have found gold on Little Minook Creek about 1893." (See Donald Orth's *Dictionary of Alaska Place Names*, 1971, Washington, Government Printing Office, U.S. Geological Survey Professional Paper 567, p. 646.) Mynook and Manook are variations of the spelling.

28. F E stands for Fairbanks Exploration Company a large mining company still operating in the Fairbanks area. A pipe walker is a person who checks the steam pipes used to thaw the ground. He walks through the field of thaw pipes and repairs those that are leaking. In mining operations the ground is thawed and overburden is removed until the miners reach the gold-bearing gravels.

29. In the early days, the pattern for trappers was to head up by boat to their trapping cabins in the fall before freeze-up. At Christmas time they would come into town or the village to trade some of their winter's catch. They'd be back out to the trapline till after break-up, when they would bring in fur and go to fish camp. This pattern changed somewhat when schools were established in the towns and villages. Then family members were split up for most of the winter.

30. Dried fish was an important part of the diet, for both people and dogs.

31. Before completion of the Alaska Railroad, supplies were shipped up from Seattle to Nome and St. Michael and transported by riverboat up the Yukon River. When the railroad was completed then some supplies were freighted in by rail to Nenana and loaded on steamboats for transport to villages along the Yukon, Koyukuk, and Tanana Rivers.

32. Steamboats had safes and the pursers handled money for passengers.

33. Old Adam was the father of Solomon Adams who was Moses' brother-in-law.

34. Wiseman was a gold mining community that developed on the upper Koyukuk River. Although there were earlier strikes, the discoveries in 1899 prompted a rush of prospectors to the Koyukuk. Prospectors represented many different ethnic backgrounds. Kobuk Eskimos like Sam Pingalo and his family were attracted to the area and they found work hauling freight, hunting, and prospecting. For more information on Wiseman see Robert Marshall's *Arctic Village*, 1933, New York, Harrison, Smith, and Robert Haas.

35. Paul Gagnon was Executive Director of the Alaska Rural Development Authority. (See *The Beaver Report*, 1959, Juneau, Alaska Rural Development Board.)

36. This is the Alaska Highway. Built by the military in 1942 to facilitate the northern defense, the highway stretches from Dawson Creek, British Columbia to Fairbanks, a distance of 1,420 miles. (See Claus Naske and Herman Slotnick's *Alaska: A History of the 49th State*, 1979, Grand Rapids, William B. Eerdmans Publishing Company, p. 118-119.)

37. Wannigans are small cabins built on skids so they can be easily moved.

38. Venetie is a village on the Chandalar River, roughly halfway between Beaver and Arctic Village.

39. BIA stands for the Bureau of Indian Affairs.

40. Before his retirement in 1976, Moses had worked 19 years for the BIA school in Beaver.

41. The Fairbanks Native Association (FNA) was established in 1963 to meet the needs of Alaska Natives living in Fairbanks. Over the years, the Association has developed programs in the fields of health and education. Moses works with pre-schoolers in the Parent-Child Center, FNA Education Department.

42. For Athabaskan groups living in areas even more remote from the fur traders and the early gold seekers, there was a long period of time, perhaps as much as seventy-five to a hundred years, in which they knew about the newcomers and their useful goods but had little if any direct contact with them. Then in the early years of this century the stampeders spilled over from the Yukon into the upper Kuskokwim, Tanana, and Copper rivers.

43. Captain Ray of the U.S. Army was sent to the Interior of Alaska in 1897 to investigate reports of hardships for prospectors and stampeders in the Yukon Valley. One of his findings was that the Indians on the Porcupine River were suffering because they could not acquire supplies from the traders. This was because the supplies were being controlled by the transportation companies and local traders often could not obtain them. When they could get supplies the prices were very high. (See P.H. Ray's letter to Adjutant-General, United States Army, January 5, 1898 reported in *Compilation of Narratives of Explorations in Alaska*, 1900, Washington, Government Printing Office, p. 551.)

    Athabaskan elder Belle Herbert from Chalkyitsik also reports on this starvation. (See Bill Pfisterer's book, *Shandaa: In My Lifetime*, 1982, Fairbanks, Alaska Native Language Center, University of Alaska, Fairbanks, p. 126-127.)

44. Terrence Cole has written a very interesting account of the founding of Fairbanks. (See his book, *E.T. Barnette: The Strange Story of the Man Who Founded Fairbanks*, 1981, Anchorage, Alaska Northwest Publishing Company.)

45. An account of the history of Beaver is available in William Schneider's dissertation, *Beaver, Alaska: The Story of a Multi-Ethnic Community*.

46. Hudson Stuck provides a good discussion of the history of the Episcopal Church in Alaska in his book, *The Alaskan Missions of the Episcopal Church*, 1920, New York, Domestic and Foreign Missionary Society. The reference to Dr. Burke is from p. 161.

47. This quote is from Hudson Stuck's book, *Ten Thousand Miles With a Dog Sled*, 1914, New York, Charles Scribner's Sons, p. 356.

48. This point has been made by Gary Holthaus and Ray Collins in the article, "Education in the North: Its Effect on Athapascan Culture." in *Northian*, Vol. 8, no. 4.

49. Fairbanks banker William Stroecker has provided perspective on the evolution of Fairbanks from camp to town in a recording now available at the Archives, Alaska and Polar Regions Department, Elmer Rasmuson Library, University of Alaska, Fairbanks. Tape # H-85-12.

50. For those people interested in pursuing this topic they may enjoy Marvin R. "Muktuk" Marston's book, *Men of the Tundra; Eskimos at War*, 1969, New York, October House Inc. Moses' military experience actually began when he was a student at Mt. Hermon School. He spent the summers at Camp Plattsburg in New York, a military training camp. He was provided room and board and a small salary.

51. For a discussion of the connection between housing and tuberculosis see Paul Gagnon's *The Beaver Report*, p.11. Dr. Earl Albrecht has provided detail on the history of medical efforts in Alaska to eradicate tuberculosis. (See Tape # H-85-3 and # H-86-30(A & B) at the Archives, Alaska and Polar Regions Department, Elmer Rasmuson Library, University of Alaska, Fairbanks.)

52. Under the 1971 Alaska Native Claims Settlement Act, villagers were given the opportunity to choose land for their communities to own and manage. Throughout Alaska, Indians, Eskimos, and Aleuts struggled with the new law which promised economic opportunities but also threatened to erode their intimate historic relationship with the land. The National Interest Lands refers to those areas set aside in the Alaska Native Claims Settlement Act (ANCSA) for the federal agencies to manage. The lands are referenced in 17(D)(2) of ANCSA. The management directions were finally mandated in the Alaska National Interest Lands Conservation Act (ANILCA) in 1980. For more information on ANCSA, see Robert Arnold's book, *Alaska Native Land Claims*, 1978, Anchorage, Alaska Native Foundation.

53. The recently completed Alaska Native Review Commission Report, *Village Journey* (September 1985), is a reflection of the continuing interest in assessing the impacts of legislative and economic developments on Alaska Natives living in rural Alaska. This report has been published. (See Thomas Berger's *Village Journey: The Report of the Alaska Native Review Commission*, 1985, New York, Hill and Wong.)

54. The distinction between life story and life history is summarized by Jeff Todd Titon in "The Life Story," *Journal of American Folklore*, July, 1980, Vol.93, no.369, p.276-292.

55. The folklorist, Alan Dundes, suggests that folklore analysis in general can be strengthened by attention to texture, text, and context. By *texture* he means the specific language used, the appeal of phrases like "...powerful dog, wide chest, flopped eared, old worker from way back, that one." By *text* he means that particular version of a story that is told, for instance, my choosing one of two versions of the story about prospecting with Sam Pingalo. *Context* refers to the setting in which the story is told, the people present, what has gone on preceeding the telling, and even the place where the story is told. In this book the texture is, in large part, preserved. The text is selectively preserved although, in cases where there are several versions of a story, I have combined details from each to enrich the account. Unfortunately, with the exception of a few comments about public meetings and work with students at the Fairbanks Native Association, the reader learns very little about the context in which these stories are told. Dundes' article, "Texture, Text, and Context," appeared in *Southern Folklore Quarterly, Vol. 28, (1964), p.251-265.*

56. Even with these kinds of considerations in mind, you can never be sure how one's work is received. I thought at first that the story of Turak Newman, *One Man's Trail*, wasn't received very well. For a long time I didn't really know how Turak liked what I had done with his words. Then a year ago I was talking to a group of nurses and one said that she used to provide patient care in Beaver. She told of one old man there who gave her a copy of a book on his life. As she told about this man showing her the book, pointing out the stories, and retelling some of them, tears came to my eyes because I knew that the old man was Turak Newman, and I realized for the first time that he was pleased with the book.

PHOTOGRAPHIC CREDITS

(Photographs listed by page number.)

iv. Dedication of the Cruikshank School, Beaver, Alaska. Photograph by Dan Gullickson.

vii. Moses and Ruth Cruikshank at the Athabaskan Old Time Fiddler's Festival in Fairbanks, 1984. Photograph by Rob Stapleton.

13. Hudson's Bay Company freight boats. Historical Photograph Collection, Archives, University of Alaska, Fairbanks (acc. # 75-209-97).

17. Mrs. Grafton Burke. Elizabeth Hayes Goddard Collection, Archives, University of Alaska, Fairbanks.

19. The river steamboat *Yukon*. Edby Davis Collection, Archives, University of Alaska, Fairbanks (acc. # 73-190-219).

21. Episcopal Mission, Nenana. Ben Mozee Collection, Archives, University of Alaska, Fairbanks (acc. # 79-26-782).

29. The *Pelican.* Walter and Lillian Phillips Album, Episcapol Church Collection, Archives, University of Alaska, Fairbanks (acc. # 85-072).

40. Deaconess Bedell and Henry Moses and his wife Mabel. Episcopal Church Collection, Archives, University of Alaska, Fairbanks.

43. Bill and Herman Yanert. Fabian Carey Collection, Archives, University of Alaska, Fairbanks (acc. # 75-209-50).

44. Purgatory, Alaska. Elizabeth Hayes Goddard Collection (1934), Archives, University of Alaska, Fairbanks.

46. Moses and Ruth Cruikshank with Ruth's father Turak Newman. Photograph by Robert Cruikshank.

52. The old Pioneer Hotel. Charles Bunnell Collection, Archives, University of Alaska, Fairbanks (acc. # 63-46-20).

53. The Model Cafe. Archie Lewis Collection, Archives, University of Alaska, Fairbanks (acc. # 896-66).

54. Travelling sleds. Fabian Carey Collection, Archives, University of Alaska, Fairbanks (acc. #75-209-97).

56. Surfacing crew building the old Alaska Railroad. Frederick Mears Collection, Archives, University of Alaska, Fairbanks (acc. # 84-75-39).

57. Work horses and mules. Frederick Mears Collection, Archives, University of Alaska, Fairbanks (acc. # 84-75-308).

58. Railroad crew laying rails. Frederick Mears Collection, Archives, University of Alaska, Fairbanks (acc. # 84-75-8).

61. The Miller family. Photograph from Moses Cruikshank's personal collection.

63. The Working *Pelican*. Photograph from Moses Cruikshank's personal collection.

65. St. Mathews Mission. Guilbert Thompson Collection, Archives, University of Alaska, Fairbanks (acc. # 67-42-6).

66. St. John in the Wilderness Church, Allakaket. Elizabeth Goddard Collection (1934), Archives, University of Alaska, Fairbanks.

89. Camp on the Hodzana. Photograph by Robert Cruikshank. Moses Chuikshank Collection, University of Alaska, Fairbanks (acc # 85-100-01).

95. Old Adam. Photograph from the personal collection of Charlotte Adams.

98. Celia Hunter with Moses and his wife, Ruth and two of their children, Charlotte and Robert. Photograph from Moses Cruikshank Collection, University of Alaska, Fairbanks (acc # 85-100-09).

101. Ambrose Williams and Moses with the cat train leaving Beaver in March 1959. Photographed by John Melville. Record Group 315, Alaska Development Board, 1955-1959, Series 107, Box 1143, file "Village Rehabilitation Program, Arctic Village, July 1957-April 1960." Alaska State Archives, Juneau.

102. Moses and Clinton Wiehl, the "Cat" man, with the cat train leaving Beaver, March 1959. Photographed by John Melville. Record Group 315, Alaska Development Board, 1955-1959, Series 107, Box 1143, file "Village Rehabilitation Program, Arctic Village, July 1957-April 1960." Alaska State Archives, Juneau.

108. Moses Cruikshank with class from Parent- Child Center, Fairbanks Native Association. Photograph by S.V. Cowdrey, (acc # 827/40, FNA/JOM).

112. Moses Cruikshank and William Schneider recording at the Elmer Rasmuson Library, Library Staff Photograph Collection.

116. Archdeacon Stuck. Episcopal Church Collection, Archives, University of Alaska, Fairbanks.

120. Moses Cruikshank. Photograph by S.V. Cowdrey, (acc # 608/41A-42, FNA/JOM).

ACKNOWLEDGEMENTS

There are many people who have influenced the development of this book but the most important is Dr. Margaret Blackman. She thoroughly reviewed the first draft and her comments were invaluable. In an exciting and positive way, her criticisms have led me to re-examine basic questions about how life histories are written. Her observations served as a springboard for comments from Bill Brown, Gary Holthaus, and T. Neil Daivs.

Dan O'Neill made a generous contribution of time and skill by suggesting editorial changes. Jean Lester edited the entire manuscript several times and Sidney Stephens helped revise several chapters and provided support throughout the project.

Paul McCarthy, head of the Alaska & Polar Regions Department at the Elmer Rasmuson Library, University of Alaska, Fairbanks has generously supported the entire project including reproduction of photographs, copying of texts, and typing. Cyndee Simpson was the key person who actually produced the manuscript, first from cut and pasted copy and then through several revisions, and she kept smiling the whole way. Linda Thomas made the final corrections. Nancy Brown researched photo collections and hard-to-find details for the footnotes.

Some of the photographs are from the Fairbanks Native Association and their staff photographer, S.V. Cowdrey, copied selected photos for this publication. Robert Cruikshank's photographs from summer trips with his father add a visual dimension to the descriptions of the Hodzana. Photographs depicting the Rural Development Project are from the Alaska State Archives in Juneau and were researched by Deputy State Archivist, Virginia Newton.

Book design and layout was done by Jan Steinbright and the staff of the Institute of Alaska Native Arts with funding assistance from the University of Alaska Press. Cheryl Cline did final proof reading and made valuable suggestions.

Publication funds were provided by the National Endowment for the Humanities and the Alaska Humanities Forum. I am particularly appreciative of their support for this project.

Many thanks to each of these people. The book has benefited from their generous help.